CODE MAKING
AND
CODE BREAKING

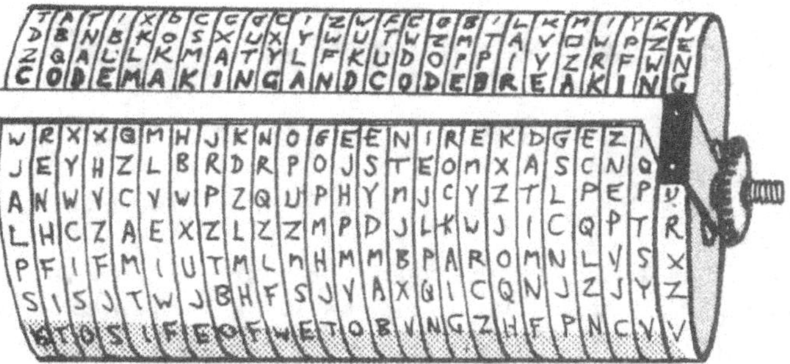

Jack Luger

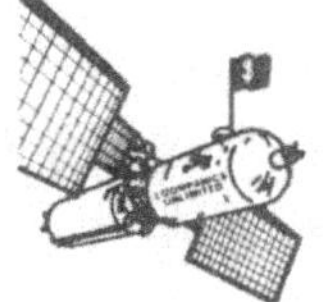

Loompanics Unlimited
Port Townsend, Washington

Jack Luger is the author of these fine books available from Loompanics Unlimited:

- *Improvised Weapons in American Prisons*
- *How to Use Mail Drops for Privacy and Profit*
- *Counterfeit I.D. Made Easy*
- *The Big Book of Secret Hiding Places*

Contents

1

Introduction

This is a practical handbook on how to make your own codes and how to "break" other peoples' codes. You'll find enough theory in this book to give you a good background regarding how and why codes work, but the emphasis is on practical topics so that you can put this knowledge to work as quickly as possible.

It's necessary to skim over the history and development of codes and ciphers, to place the subject in perspective and to provide indications of what's been tried before. Some efforts failed miserably, while others were unqualified successes. Some "crypto" efforts affected history. We don't know about many of these efforts because governments are very secretive regarding their crypto work. Most of what's going on today in the many cryptographic struggles between governments affects us directly and indirectly, but is likely to remain secret during our lifetimes.

There's a very definite and solid reason why cryptographic secrets are the most closely-guarded, even more than those involving nuclear weapons. Anyone who manages to steal nuclear weapons information has only that. Everything else in the secret world is still locked away from him. With the codes and ciphers, he has access to all secret communications. This enables penetrating the secrecy surrounding many areas. However, the areas that governments choose to keep secret may surprise some. For example, there's absolutely no secret about the "unbreakable" code or cipher. These exist, and the technology for producing them has been with us for at least six decades. Many governments use unbreakable ciphers.

Code-breaking, or cryptanalysis, as we shall see, is the most secret activity of all. The ability to "read" another country's traffic is priceless in many cases, and governments not only jealously guard their techniques, but the very fact that they have them.

Codes have been in use for thousands of years. If there's a need to keep a secret, someone will think of a way to record it so that it can't be read by those not in the know. Some of the people who invented codes were naive, and didn't realize that what seemed to be an unbreakable code to them was simple for another to crack wide open. At the time, however, most people were illiterate, and anything written was incomprehensible to them. Those who could read were very unsophisticated regarding codes and ciphers, and consequently many simple-minded ciphers were secure from the opposition.

Today, with the experience of centuries to guide us, we can avoid many common mistakes. We also have some new technical aids which were unavailable only a few years ago, and which, when properly used, can make codes extremely difficult to break.

Not all codes are equally easy to decipher. The major factor in the decision to adopt a particular system is not whether or not it's absolutely unbreakable, but whether the opposition has the ability to break it, or whether they can break it in time to do them any good.

The secret penetrators in our society have been well-documented. Private parties snoop on individuals. Governments snoop on individuals and on each other. Organizations, such as employers and labor unions, use espionage and various forms of wiretapping and electronic "bugging" to intercept communications. Any radio transmission can be overheard.

If you have a need to keep your communications secret, read tins book carefully. In these pages you'll find a description of many practical systems for hiding the meanings of your messages. You'll find a description and objective appraisal of each

«nil*. Some are very secure, but hard to use. Others require costly equipment, and we won't waste much time with these. Still others are workable if your opponent's not too bright, but no good against a sophisticated adversary. A few offer good security and case of use. With this array, you should have no problem in setting up a code system to meet your needs. This is a nut- and-bolts book, designed to allow the reader to start off with as little difficulty as possible.

This is why many of the exotic ciphers and codes are not in this book. We'll discuss briefly various electro-mechanical encryption machines, but keep in mind that they're practical only lor governments and corporations because of their high cost.

Some of these beautifully intricate crypto-systems are too elaborate and cumbersome to be practical. The mathematical "gateing" equations are elegant, but truly impractical for the down and dirty conditions in which most of us have to use secrecy. Likewise, there are encryption and decryption methods adaptable to the home computer, but not everyone has a computer or the knowledge to use one in a way suitable for cryptography. In any case, this information is available elsewhere.

There is no glossary of technical terms here. If you're new to the subject, read the chapters in sequence and you'll find the technical terms explained as we come to them. It's better this way, because you'll get the definitions in context with the explanations.

The bottom line is that it's much easier to set up a crypto-system than to break one. This is why we'll devote more time and space to discuss codes and ciphers than to explaining how to break them.

Devising a nearly unbreakable code is easy, although not as easy as some people think. However, with a little intelligent effort, you'll be able to set up your own code or cipher and make it secure enough so that it will be extremely difficult for even the most sophisticated code-breaker to unlock.

2

History

We study history to learn from it. We can draw some valuable lessons from the cryptographic mistakes of the past.

We don't have to examine the history of codes and ciphers in nit-picking detail. What's important is the way that codes and ciphers fitted into the needs of their users. The history of cryptography is closely intertwined with the history of communication, and we'll see that, as means of communication increased, so did the need for keeping certain messages secret.

Codes and ciphers, with one exception, are worthwhile only to those who need to keep secrets. This usually means governments, because of their diplomatic and military branches, and private individuals and organizations engaged in intrigues. The reason why military organizations need to keep their secrets is obvious. Diplomats often use mis-representations and under-the- table deals to further their countries' ends, and for this reason need to keep their communications secret.

The exception noted above has to do with brevity. In various types of transmission and record-keeping, there's a real need to use symbols to save space or time. A conspicuous example of this is the group of "telegraph codes" which came about shortly after the telegraph became wide-spread. Telegrams are charged by the word, and a commercial code book which uses five or six letter code words to represent phrases and even sentences can save a company a lot of money in transmission costs. The code books are in no way secret, and are available on the open market.

Likewise, the various systems of "short-hand" are codes or ciphers, but because anyone can learn them by buying a book or taking a class, they're not secret. They allow a secretary to take dictation without having to write every letter or word.

We also see codes used in radio traffic for the same reason. Police channels are crowded, and during peak hours it's important to reduce the length of messages to accommodate the large number of users. Thus, " 10-28" stands for "check license plate number with the Motor Vehicle Department" and " 10-29" means "check this person or vehicle for outstanding warrants."

In ancient times, when practically nobody knew how to read or write, messages were verbal. A military commander would send a courier, and security of the message depended on the courier's ability to make it safely to his destination. If captured by the enemy, he simply had to keep his mouth shut. His captors might not even realize that he was a courier, but might assume that he was a simple soldier or even a deserter.

Written messages also depended heavily on the courier's skill for security. Their senders often did not bother to encipher them for this reason. Sometimes, they miscalculated. The capture of the British courier, Major John Andre, by American forces during the Revolutionary War had serious consequences because of the material he was carrying. It led to the exposure of Benedict Arnold as a traitor.

Couriers allowed the sender to direct the message very precisely. To intercept the message, it was imperative to intercept the courier, and this wasn't easy to do. The electronic explosion changed this drastically. At first, the telegraph was vulnerable to anyone who had access to the line. It was impossible to guard every telegraph wire over every foot of its length, and anyone with crude equipment could tap into the line and read the messages. Use of the telegraph during the

American Civil War Ini to the first widespread use of codes and ciphers in warfare.

It wasn't the first American effort in truly secure crypto communication, though. Many years before, the third American President, Thomas Jefferson, invented a ciphering device based on polyalphabetical substitution. This was the basic device upon which many recent American devices are based, and the development of this device led to the electro-mechanical cipher machines developed in the years between the two world wars.

Radio made it worse for the sender, who spread his message over a wide area. The eavesdropper didn't need to touch or even come close to his target's equipment, but could pick up his messages from thousands of miles away under favorable conditions. With direction-finding gear, he could estimate the location of the transmitter. This was valuable for locating enemy ships. This is why a German general said, during World War II, that use of the radio was treason.

The growth of cryptology was also a result of the growth of military and "intelligence" services. With larger armies and navies, as well as the beginning of a new service, the air force, there were more messages to send, and the pressure of time made them more urgent. Modern intelligence services, unlike the old espionage services, tend to stress technical means of information- gathering over human factors. This is because they've learned to deduce important facts about their enemies from intercepting their communications. Direction-finding equipment located enemy transmitters. Listing and analyzing the contents of messages disclosed information about the location, strength, and plans of enemy forces. A request for an ammunition resupply, lor example, would suggest a coming offensive if it was larger than normal. Casualty reports would show how enemy strength had declined after a battle.

With the realization that any scrap of information could help an enemy eavesdropper, there arose a system of information classification, and a system of codes and ciphers to transmit various types of information. The most secure codes and ciphers were for top-secret messages between various military headquarters. Less complex and presumably, less secure, systems were for routine administrative traffic and for front-line units that might be overrun and their codes captured.

The very simple "field ciphers" were for small units, and they were not very secure. In many cases, pessimistic estimates of their difficulty were that a competent code-cracker could undo them within hours. This was enough, for by the time a crypt-analyst decoded a message, its information would be obsolete.

Messages of extreme importance, compromise of which would be a national disaster, still went by courier. So did de-liveries of new crypto systems. This is still true today. The diplomatic pouch is a conduit for codes, cipher machines, and related security gear.

Although a human courier sometimes is still vulnerable to capture, sending the message by radio in a possibly insecure crypto system is far worse because an enemy could record and de-crypt it without the sender's knowledge. There have been many instances during our century when a government did not know that an enemy or rival was reading its most secret messages.

In the following pages we'll study how certain types of crypto- systems fit into various contexts. We'll see how codebreakers worked to unlock their secrets, while code-makers scurried to create more secure codes and ciphers.

3

Secret Writing: The Basics

Let's begin by laying out the difference between a "code" and a "cipher." A code involves using code words, symbols, or groups of numbers to replace words or phrases in the original message, or "plaintext." For example, in a military code book, we might find that "GFRDS" stands for "Attack" and "HJUYN" stands for "Attack immediately." Also very common are number groups of five or six digits.

A cipher works with the elements of a message, the individual letters. A "substitution" cipher uses another letter or a number h, represent each letter of the alphabet. A "transposition" cipher scrambles a message in a systematic way that only the recipient can understand.

In this volume, we'll try to maintain technical accuracy, but sometimes it's not worth the effort. When dealing with individual codes and ciphers, we'll use the proper terms because otherwise we'd cause confusion. In general discussions, however, it's not necessary to try for technical perfection. For example, when we speak of a nation's "diplomatic codes," we include both codes and ciphers. Likewise, the term "codebreaker" doesn't mean a person who breaks only codes and leaves ciphers alone. The term "crypto system" can apply to codes, ciphers, or mixtures of both. We speak of a secret message being "encrypted" when we mean one or the other, without being specific. In code-breaking, for example, the technician works with encrypted messages, and his first task is to find out how they were encrypted. The "crypto system" might be code, cipher, or both.

As we study various code and cipher systems, we'll find that, in practical use, there are many mixed crypto systems. A simple substitution cipher is easy to crack, but when mixed with a transposition, the difficulty for the code-cracker is increased out of proportion. Likewise, many nations using a code book will safeguard against casual penetration by enciphering their code groups.

MESSAGE CONCEALMENT

There's one general type of secret writing that's not really a code or cipher but depends upon concealment. There are many techniques of concealing secret writing, from secret compartments in ordinary objects to microdots. We'll run through these briefly.

SECRET INKS

There are many chemicals which will produce colorless ink that becomes visible when developed with another chemical. Iron sulfate produces colorless writing, until the addressee develops it with a solution of potassium cyanate, when it turns blue. Copper sulfate forms blue crystals that dissolve to become a colorless ink. Treating the paper with ammonia fumes brings out the secret writing in red.

Phenolphthalein is the active ingredient in EX-LAX® and other laxatives. It's also available in tablets and as a white, taste-less powder that's hard to dissolve in pure water. Mixing one tablet of phenolphthalein with half an ounce of ammonia water and an ounce of water gives a colorless ink that becomes visible when treated with sodium carbonate or other alkalis.

Some secret inks develop by heat. Milk, for example, will turn brown when the paper is heated. A solution of one part alum to 100 parts water provides an ink that shows when the paper is heated with a hot iron. So does writing with a sugar solution.

This purpose of invisible ink is to avoid showing that the message even exists. Practical use involves writing an innocent letter to the addressee and writing the secret message on the back or between the lines. In so doing, it's important to avoid tell-tale notches on the paper. This is why people using secret inks are careful to apply it only with a ballpoint pen or, more commonly, cotton swab. This is to avoid scratching the paper as a conventional pen nib does. The disturbed paper fibers are visible under a magnifying glass.

It the writer uses cotton swabs, he can't use too much liquid on the paper will swell and buckle. If he's writing on paper with unmatched "sizing," the texture of the coating will be disturbed. Yet another way to use a secret ink is to soak another sheet of paper with the ink and to let it dry. When dry, the writer uses it as a secret ink "carbon paper," sandwiching it with the letter so that when he writes on it the ink will press off onto the paper underneath. Another, slower way is to write on a blank sheet of paper and sandwich, it with another, allowing ambient moisture to transfer the writing to the second sheet. This requires pressing both sheets together under a stack of books for many hours.

There are several ways of detecting secret writing. One is to use a cage device with several brushes or swabs in a row, each with a different developing chemical. This technique, used during WWII, would sometimes disclose secret inks.1[1]

Working on the disturbed fibers in the paper seems to be the most promising way to detect secret inks, and sometimes applying iodine fumes will make them show. British scientists have developed a "universal developer," using radioactivity. which detects many secret inks. [2]

Another problem with secret inks is the physical paraphernalia required. A secret agent who tries to bring the materials in with him risks exposure by alert customs officials and counter- espionage agents who normally frequent ports of entry. A set consisting of a vial of chemical and some cotton applicators al- most screams, "secret ink," which is why there have been serious efforts to disguise such chemicals. The chemical can be put into solution, used to saturate an article of clothing such as a handkerchief, and allowed to dry. German agents devised this technique during WWI. Only a rigorous examination would reveal secret ink concealed this way. Having the secret ink on a pad of paper which the agent uses for "carbons" is another solution. The best is for the agent to obtain the chemicals in- country. There are many commonly available materials useful for this.

GRILLS

A grill can be an actual paper grill, or a simple system such as using every tenth word as the actual message. Let's say that our message is "COME AT ONCE." If we use a system, such as

---

[1] *Secret Warfare: The Battle of Codes and Ciphers*, Bruce Norman, NY, Dorset Press, 1973, p. 93.

[2] *Spy-Catcher*, Peter Wright, NY, Dell Books, 1988, p. 149

making every tenth word the message and filling in the spaces, we might get a result like this:

"Dear John;
I tried to ask Mama not to COME, but I couldn't reach her. See, she was not AT home. It's true that I tried much more than ONCE."

Using every tenth word makes for a very long letter, and some will designate every fifth or sixth word. This is more awkward, and often results in strange phrasing.

A paper or cardboard template with slots for the location of the hidden words is shown in Figure 1.

DEAR JOHN,
I TRIED TO ASK MAMA NOT TO COME, BUT I COULDN'T REACH
HER, SEE, SHE WAS NOT AT HOME. IT'S TRUE THAT I
TRIED MUCH MORE THAN ONCE.

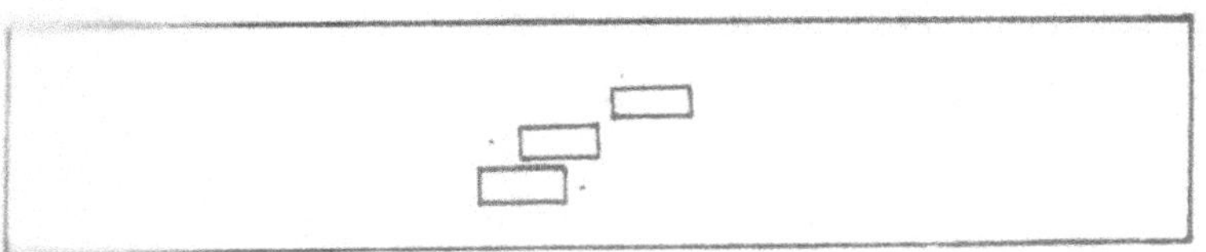

DEAR JOHN,
I TRIED TO ASK MAMA NOT TO **COME**, BUT I COULDN'T REACH
HER, SEE, SHE WAS NOT **AT** HOME. IT'S TRUE THAT I
TRIED MUCH MORE THAN **ONCE**.

FIGURE 1

A template grill has holes where code words appear.

This shows why we almost never see grills anymore. The slots are of fixed sizes, but words vary in length. This makes a grill very y awkward to use. We'll look at an ingenious one in the transposition cipher chapter, though.

OPEN CODE

Less awkward to use is the open or jargon code, which uses innocuous and ordinary words to denote important data. A letter written by a spy to his controller might read this way:

"Last week, I went on a trip into the country. Along the way to the farm, 120 miles southeast of my home, I saw 3 cows strolling along the road. At the farm, there were another dozen cows, about 100 horses, and two dozen mules."

In this code, "cow" stands for tanker aircraft, "horse" means fighter, and "mule" stands for bomber. The farm is obviously an air base, located 120 miles southeast of whatever reference point the spy calls "home."

THE PINHOLE CIPHER

One way of sending a concealed message is almost totally out of use today, although it's very simple. This involves pricking a pin-hole in each letter making up a message on a printed page. The message can be concealed in a magazine, for example, and when the addressee receives it, he simply looks for the article with pin-holes in some of the letters. To help him, the sender can prick a hole in front of the title on the table of contents.

The problem with this technique is that anyone looking for it will find it quickly by running his fingertips across the page. This is an old trick and probably every counter-espionage agent and customs officer in the world knows about it.

MESSAGES DISGUISED IN ORAWINGS

According to legend, Robert Baden-Powell used drawings to conceal diagrams of military fortifications as he scouted for the British Empire. He adopted the disguise of a butterfly collector and, equipped with a net, pencils, and pad of paper, noted the details of enemy forts and drew them into the drawings of butterfly wings.

Another old dodge is the architectural or landscape drawing. Another example is shown below in Figure 2. This illustration shows how it's possible to conceal the dots and dashes of a coded message as blades of grass. Although this was a workable code for its day, not everyone can draw well enough to make a passable drawing, and the time involved makes this technique impractical.

FIGURE 2

Drawings are one way of conveying a secret message.
The blades of grass are actually morse code.

MICRODOTS

German scientists devised this system for use in World War II. The "microdot" is a tiny disc of fine-grain, high-resolution microfilm which contains a page of writing, visible only with extreme magnification. A microdot looks like a small and shiny black disc, about 1/32" in diameter. With a tiny dab of glue, it fits at the end of a sentence where a period would be and will pass casual inspection. Yet, anyone looking at the paper under strong light might, if the light strikes it right, wonder why one of the periods is shiny. Some operators hid the microdot under the envelope flap or under the postage stamp. Indeed, the microdot's tiny size made it possible to hide almost anywhere.

Making microdots requires a special camera and film to photograph the pages. Careful developing yields a negative which the operator has to cut out of the film frame with a special tool that looks like a tiny hole punch. Reading a microdot requires either a microscope or a special enlarger to bring the image back to normal size. Often, the sender gains extra security by not using "clear," or plaintext, but encrypting his message. This is an extra obstacle for anyone who finds the microdot.

Concealment systems have very little going for them, and several drawbacks, which is why they're rarely used today. One problem is that they can take too long to arrive. A letter to another country can take weeks in transit, while a radio signal is instantaneous. Another is that some require special equipment which can be compromising in some situations. Materials for secret inks are hard to explain away during a customs search. A set of lenses and tools for making microdots suggests "spy" very strongly.

SEEKING A CODE

There's no ideal means of secret communication. All have some drawbacks, but some are better than others. Let's look at some desirable qualities of codes and ciphers before we look at specific examples.

A very important point is simplicity. There are some practically unbreakable codes and ciphers that are so awkward that you need a Ph.D. in mathematics to understand them. A code or cipher system is likely to be used by ordinary people, often working under stress. Simplicity helps.

Another advantage of simplicity is saving time. A cipher that requires an hour's work to encipher a few sentences isn't cost-effective. The sender may not be able to afford the time. It also slows downturn-around time, if the sender needs a reply.

The system should require no equipment or compromising documents if the person is going to be doing anything clandestine. A code book or a cipher machine causes no problem aboard a warship or at a military base, but if the user is going to undertake a secret mission, either is a liability. This is the same problem as with secret inks or microdots. As we'll see, there are some ways of reducing the size of or otherwise disguising code keys.

It's also helpful if the system is error-free or fairly immune to error. Enciphering messages is difficult enough, and subject to errors. Some systems, such as the "autokey" cipher, allow no error at all. A single mistake, by the person who enciphers, transmits or receives the message, will make it total garble. A good system doesn't absolutely prevent errors, but the effect only wipes out one word or phrase, not the entire message.

Secret writing is a discipline in itself, almost like another culture. It requires a different way of thinking.

CONVENTIONS IN SECRET WRITING

The purpose is to confound unauthorized persons trying to read the message. A basic principle is to avoid giving the code-breaker any help, such as punctuation or word breaks. No modern cipher has any punctuation marks in the ciphertext.

Likewise, no modern code or cipher leaves any part of the message in clear. A couple of centuries ago, secret agents used short codes to disguise the meanings of critical phrases. A message thus might read: "Meet me at 36485." This system offered very little security, despite the high hopes of the code's compiler, because it disclosed several elements of the message while concealing only one.

Another step is to break up all of the text into five-letter or five-number groups. This is to hide word breaks and to mimic codes. It makes a code-breaker's task tougher if he has to struggle to determine whether he's dealing with a code or cipher, and since it's customary to use five-letter groups in codes, arranging ciphertext in similar groups helps.

Another convention is to use "nulls," or meaningless letters or numbers, to fill out the text. To make even groups, it's important to have a certain word or letter count. If there are only a few spaces to fill, several Xs will do. Longer spaces require more letters, and some cipher clerks use their imaginations to fill the spaces. Some use common quotations, such as the Pledge of Allegiance, or the Lord's Prayer. Others may use poetry. One cipher clerk who did caused a classic misunderstanding.

In the Pacific Theater during WWII, Admiral Halsey had created a sub-unit of his Third Fleet, called "Task Force 34." During the Battle of Leyte Gulf, Admiral Kincaid sent a message to Halsey, asking him where Task Force 34 was, as he needed its support. The Commander in Chief, Pacific, Admiral Nimitz, heard this, and sent Halsey a message asking him the same thing. The cipher clerk, however, added a few words of his own to fill out a line. There are several versions of this story, but the most common one is that the clerk chose a line from Tennyson's "Charge of the Light Brigade." The message finally read:

WHERE IS TASK FORCE 34
AS ALL THE WORLD WONDERS

Halsey received the message with the nulls included because his code clerk had mistakenly thought that they were part of the message. As he read it, he thought that it was an insulting message, coming from the Pacific Commander, and he became very angry. He turned his ships around and headed South to go help Kincaid. [3]

Yet another convention is to paraphrase all messages before releasing them for publication. Winston Churchill did this in his six volume *History of the Second World War* because including the message in cleartext might have compromised British crypto-systems still in use.

---

[3] *The Code-Breakers*, David Kahn, NY, MacMilan, 1967, pp. 608-609. The text of the message, as recorded in this book, differs from other versions. Possibly because of crypto security measures, the message has been paraphrased a few times to avoid giving away the code.

4

Substitution Ciphers

As we've seen, a "substitution" cipher is one in which one letter or number stands for each letter in the message. Although this is the principle, substitution ciphers can become quite complicated, with groups of letters or numbers denoting each letter in plaintext. We'll also see that there are ways to make a code-breaker's life hell with a few simple tricks. Let's begin with the basics, though. One important principle that dominates cryptology, and which many ignore, is "K.I.S.S." It means "Keep It Simple, Stupid." A very complicated cipher can totally confound a code-breaker, but it can cause as much trouble to tle recipient.

We're also going to avoid any ciphers which use symbols. The Sherlock Holmes story, "The Adventure of the Dancing Men," has an example of such a cipher, which is best left to the fiction writer. The symbol substitution cipher may look mystifying but offers no additional security. The disadvantage is that it's harder to transmit over the telegraph, telephone, or radio.

SIMPLE SUBSTITUTIONS

A "simple substitution" is a cipher with a single letter or number replacing each letter of the plaintext. One simple cipher is this one:

A B C D E F G H I J K L M N O P Q R S T U V W X Y Z
R S T U V W X Y Z A B C D E F G H I J K L M N O P Q

This is so simple that we may even call it "simple-minded."
The cipher alphabet is simply shifted a few spaces but still in
order. With this cipher, we would encipher the plaintext "Come
at once" this way:

TFDV RK FETV

This message may appear incomprehensible, consisting
mainly of consonants, but an experienced code-cracker might
count the letter frequency and deduce that one of the three
letters which appears twice, T, F, or V, stands for the letter "E,"
the most common letter in English.

Of course, a longer message would be more helpful, because
the frequency count's likely to be less typical with short
messages.

Let's try a simple substitution cipher using numbers:

A B C D E F G H I J K L M N O P Q R S T U V W X Y Z
17 18 1920 21 22 23 24 25 26 1 2 3 4 5 6 7 8 9 10 11 12 13 14 15 16

This isn't very practical, because it offers few possibilities for
confusing a code-breaker. "Come at once" would have to be
written this way:

19-5-3-21   17-10   5-4-19-21

The dashes are necessary to prevent confusion. Without them, the addressee would have as much trouble as the code-breaker. The message would look like this enciphered:

195321 1710 541921

Someone deciphering it might start by thinking that the first "1" stands for "K," and go on to get a plaintext that begins with "KSOMLK."

JUMBLED ALPHABETS

It helps slightly if the letters comprising the cipher section are out of normal alphabetical order, instead of reading "A, B, C," etc., even if the sequence is broken at some point. One way to do it is to use a "key word" to govern the arrangement of the letters. We first write the key word and arrange the remaining letters of the alphabet behind it in order. The only strict requirement for this sort of key word is that it have no repetitions of the same letter. Using the key word "company" we get:

A B C D E F G H I J K L M N O P Q R S T U V W X Y Z
C O M P A N Y B D E F G H I J K L Q R S T U V W X Z

In this cipher, "Z" stands for itself, but this isn't a real problem. For somewhat better security, we do something else. We write the key word at the top of a block and the remaining letters below it, in rows:

C O M P A N Y
B D E F G H I
J K L Q R S T

$$U \; V \; W \; X \; Z$$

Now we lift the letters in columns and write them under the plaintext alphabet:

$$A \; B \; C \; D \; E \; F \; G \; H \; I \; J \; K \; L \; M \; N \; O \; P \; Q \; R \; S \; T \; U \; V \; W \; X \; Y \; Z$$
$$C \; B \; J \; U \; O \; D \; K \; V \; M \; E \; L \; W \; P \; F \; Q \; Y \; A \; G \; R \; Z \; N \; H \; S \; Y \; I \; T$$

All of these simple substitution ciphers share the weakness of being vulnerable to frequency count analysis. Also, the arrangement of the words provides some giveaways to the code-breaker. For example, in our original message we have the two- letter word "AT." There aren't many two-letter words in English. They're easy to remember and spot.

We can make the ciphertext message less obvious by breaking up word lengths. If we put it into five-letter groups, we get this:

$$\text{TFDVR KFETV}$$

At first sight, this could be anything. These groups could easily be from a code book, or the result of a transposition. Still, such a message is vulnerable to a frequency count.

POLYPHONIC SUBSTITUTION

The next step in producing a difficult cipher to break is the "polyphonic" cipher. There are several systems in use, but let's keep it simple and use a letter system. Each letter will have a two-letter group representing it.

A problem with "digraphs," two-letter groups, is that if one letter drops out during transmission, the entire sequence shifts out of phase, snarling the message. The addressee has to do some trial-and-error to determine which letters or letters were lost, and which represent the message as sent. To prevent confusion for the person who receives it, we'll establish the rule that the two-letter groups begin with a letter from A-L and that the second letter will always be between M-Z. We'll have several groups to represent the most common letters in English, which we already know are E, T, A, 0, N, R, I, S, and H.

Xx

With this, let's encipher the message "I need you. Come at once." We'll use a different digraph for each of the common letters to avoid building up anything that will show in a frequency count. Here's what we get:

GR EMBQHPBP GNENFO BOGTDQGQ AMFN HUIRBOJX

The only digraph which repeats is "BO," which stands for "C." Now let's make it a little more difficult by breaking the words up to foil any intuitive substitution:

GREMB QHPBP GNENF OBOGT DQGQA MFNHU IRBOJ
XMOVP

We also did something sneaky here. Note the last group. There weren't enough letters to produce an even group, and there were four spaces to fill. The trick is to add "nulls," letters that don't mean anything, to fill the spaces. The receiver will know that the last letters, "MOVP," are meaningless because they are from the second half of the alphabet, and can't begin any digraphs.

An easier cipher to construct uses a grid, and is also polyphonic. In this case, we'll also set up a couple of arbitrary rules. We'll use two-letter groups to denote each letter. We'll also say that one of the first three letters of the alphabet, A, B, and C, will always be the first letter of each digraph. This is very important to avoid the addressee's becoming confused if one letter is lost or garbled in transmission. If one digraph is unclear, he, can go on to the next one and figure out the missing letter after he completes decryption. Let's set up our grid, starting with the most common letters at the top:

Cipher Letters: ABC

Plaintext:		Cipher:	
ETA			XYZVW
ONR			PUQMI
ISH			KFGJ
BCD			IEO
FGJ			BCD
KLM			RT
PQU			AS
VWX			H
YZ			N

This provides another security measure; several choices for each high-frequency letter. To encipher, we start with the letter at the top of the column containing the letter from our message, and choose one from the right-hand set of cipher letters. We can encipher the letter "E" FIVE different ways: AX, AY, AZ AV, and AW.

Let's see how this can mess up the frequency count. We'll encipher "I need you. Come at once." again:

INEEDYOUCOMEATONCE

AKBPAYAZCIANAUCABIAQCRAVCXBYALBMBEAW

Breaking this up into five-letter groups gives us:

AKBPA YAZCI ANAUC ABIAQ CRAVC XBYAL BMBEA W

We've got one letter left over. To fill out the group, we'll add
four nulls, taken from the right-hand columns because they
cannot begin in any groups:

AKBPA YAZCI ANAUC ABIAQ CRAVC XBYAL BMBEA
WNHAS

In such a short message, there's no repetition of digraphs.
This is not an unbreakable cipher, but the five-letter groups
disguise the cipher. Also, the combination of digraphs and
suppressed common-letter frequencies will slow a code-breaker
down if he's limited to paper and pencil.

THE PLAYFAIR CIPHER

An even more secure method of polyphonic substitution is
the "Playfair" Cipher. This was the British military cipher of the
late Nineteenth Century and is fairly secure against casual code-
breaking. We start with a key word that does not repeat letters,
and write the rest of the alphabet behind it:

C	O	M	P	A
N	Y	B	D	E
F	G	H	I	K

L   Q   R   S   T
U   V   W   X   Z

What we now have is a grid of five letters by five letters. To make it come out evenly, we had to drop the "J" and decide 1hat any word containing that letter will be written with an "I."

With this, let's encipher the message "I need you. Come at once." The first step is to break it up into two-letter groups, or digraphs:

IN EX ED YO UC OM EA TO NC EX

There was one set of double letters, in the word "NEED." It was necessary to break that set up by placing an "X" between them, or we would not be able to encipher the message properly. To make the message end with a set of two letters, we also added another "X" at the end.

To encipher, we follow several rules:

If both letters of a pair fall in the same row, we replace each letter with the one to its right. For example, "MO" would become "PM." If the letters are in the same column, we replace each by the letter beneath it. The pair "YO" becomes "GY" and the pair "UC" becomes "CN." Note that in the second pair, "C" was above the "U." We simply ran back to the top of the column, so that we used the "C" to encipher the "U."

Some pairs will have letters that are not in the same row or column. "TO" is one such. We then replace the "T" (in bold) by running across the row until we're right under the column with the "O" and using that letter, which is "Q" (in parentheses). We replace the "A" by going across until we're right on top of the "T," and using the "A." To be consistent, we remember the rule always to encipher the first letter of the digraph first, no matter where it is in the grid. Thus, we always get "QA" and not "AQ."

C	O	M	P	(A)
N	Y	B	D	E
F	G	H	I	K
L	(Q)	R	S	T
U	V	W	X	Z

Working through the entire message, we get:

IN	EX	ED	YO	UC	OM	EA	TO	NC	EX
FD	DZ	NE	GY	CN	MP	KE	QA	FN	DZ

To decipher the message, we write out a grid using the key word as a guide, and work it backwards, reading to the left of letters in the same row, above letters in the same column, etc.

The strength of the Playfair Cipher is that the cipher letter for each message letter will vary according to the other letter in the pair. Looking at the first digraph, we see that "IN" is "FD." However, if it were "ON," it would come out as "CY," two completely different letters. This is a serious complication for the code breaker, who must use a digraph frequency count to break into this cipher.

THE DELASTELLE CIPHER

We can call this a "double substitution" cipher because we encipher the ciphertext as well.[4] The Delastelle starts with a 25-space grid, dropping the "J" and using the "I" for both. On top and down the left side are the digits 1 to 5. Enciphering is by the

---

[4] *Clandestine Operations*, Pierre Lorain, NY, MacMilan Publishing Company, 1983, pp. 71-72

coordinate method, first with the left column and then the digit in the top row:

	1	2	3	4	5
1	C	O	M	p	A
2	N	y	B	D	E
3	F	G	H	I	K
4	L	Q	R	S	T
S	U	V	W	X	Z

We'll encipher the usual message, but write the coordinatr· vertically:

1	NEED	YOU	COME	AT	ONCE
3	2222	2 1 5	1 1 1 2	1 4	1 2 1 2
4	1554	221	123 5	55	21 I 5

Now we generate the cipher letters by reading the coordinates horizontally.

32222215111214121241554221123555 2115

G Y Y A C O P O O L Z Q N O K Z N A

We break this up into five-letter groups:

GYYAC OPOOL ZQNOK ZNA

That left a couple of empty spaces. Rather than inserting nulls, we can set the message up in three six-letter groups as well:

GYYACO POOLZQ NOKZNA

Deciphering is the reverse of these steps. Security is about as good as the Playfair, but for maximum security it's best to use a one-time keypad.

THE CIPHER WHEEL

The cipher wheel (Figure 3) is a simple idea which can create ciphers of varying complexities. The alphabet in the outer wheel is straight-on, while the inner one is reversed. The simple way to use it is to put the two "A"s together and use the inner wheel to find substitute letters for those in the outer wheel. This is a simple substitution with no more strength than a paper-and-pencil test. However, the cipher wheel offers several different modes of use.

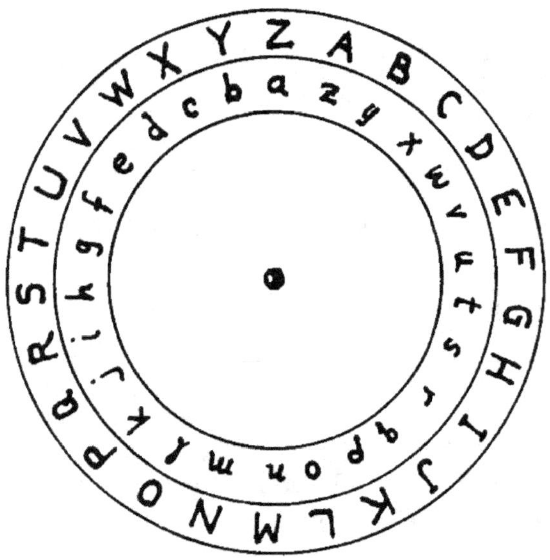

FIGURE 3

A simple cipher wheel makes it easy to
Encipher messages in a variety of ways.

The simplest one is the changing key letter. Each message can be in a different cipher, and the sender simply makes the key letter the first one of his message. The key letter is the one on the inner wheel the user places next to the "A" on the outer wheel. This provides 26 possible ciphers. Unfortunately, each individual cipher is no harder to decipher.

The key word is more difficult, and provides a true "poly-alphabetic" cipher. This is a cipher that uses more than one alphabet arrangement for enciphering, The key word's letters indicate which setting to use for each letter in the message. For example, let's set up the message; "I need you. Come at once with the key word "company:"

INEEDYO UCOMEAT O NC E

COMPANYCOMPANYCOMP

To encipher the first letter of the message, the user places the "C" of the inner wheel next to the "A" on the outer wheel. Before enciphering the "N" he sets the letter "O" next to the outer wheel's "A." This generates a different cipher. As "COMPANY" has seven letters, the message will be enciphered in seven different ciphers, creating difficulties for the code- breaker.

FIGURE 4

Similar to the cipher wheel, the cipher slide shown here is easy to make and easy to use.

The cipher slide (Figure 4) is the next gimmick which can provide the same type of changing substitutions. The main advantage of the slide is that it's easier to make neatly, requiring only a couple of pieces of paper and a typewriter. There are no problems with spacing the letters correctly around the periphery as with the cipher wheel.

All these are based upon the polyalphabet table. It looks like this:

```
A B C D E F G H I J K L M N O P Q R S T U V W X Y Z
Z A B C D E F G H I J K L M N O P Q R S T U V W X Y
Y Z A B C D E F G H I J K L M N O P Q R S T U V W X
X Y Z A B C D E F G H I J K L M N O P Q R S T U V W
W X Y Z A B C D E F G H I J K L M N O P Q R S T U V
V W X Y Z A B C D E F G H I J K L M N O P Q R S T U
U V W X Y Z A B C D E F G H I J K L M N O P Q R S T
T U V W X Y Z A B C D E F G H I J K L M N O P Q R S
S T U V W X Y Z A B C D E F G H I J K L M N O P Q R
R S T U V W X Y Z A B C D E F G H I J K L M N O P Q
Q R S T U V W X Y Z A B C D E F G H I J K L M N O P
P Q R S T U V W X Y Z A B C D E F G H I J K L M N O
O P Q R S T U V W X Y Z A B C D E F G H I J K L M N
N O P Q R S T U V W X Y Z A B C D E F G H I J K L M
M N O P Q R S T U V W X Y Z A B C D E F G H I J K L
L M N O P Q R S T U V W X Y Z A B C D E F G H I J K
K L M N O P Q R S T U V W X Y Z A B C D E F G H I J
J K L M N O P Q R S T U V W X Y Z A B C D E F G H I
I J K L M N O P Q R S T U V W X Y Z A B C D E F G H
H I J K L M N O P Q R S T U V W X Y Z A B C D E F G
G H I J K L M N O P Q R S T U V W X Y Z A B C D E F
F G H I J K L M N O P Q R S T U V W X Y Z A B C D E
E F G H I J K L M N O P Q R S T U V W X Y Z A B C D
```

DEFGHIJKLMNOPQRSTUVWXYZABC
CDEFGHIJKLMNOPQRSTUVWXYZAB
BCDEFGHIJKLMNOPQRSTUVWXYZA

Here we have 26 possible ciphers. We can use these singly, or
with a key word. Let's try a simple one, using the keyword
"LOVE."

a b c d E f g h i j k L m n O p q r s t u V w x y z

A   ABCDEFGHIJKLMNOPQRSTUVWXYZ
B   ZABCDEFGHIJKLMNOPQRSTUVWXY
C   YZABCDEFGHIJKLMNOPQRSTUVWX
D   XYZABCDEFGHIJKLMNOPQRSTUVW
E   WXYZABCDEFGHIJKLMNOPQRSTUV
F   VWXYZABCDEFGHIJKLMNOPQRSTU
G   UVWXYZABCDEFGHIJKLMNOPQRST
H   TUVWXYZABCDEFGHIJKLMNOPQRS
I   STUVWXYZABCDEFGHIJKLMNOPQR
J   RSTUVWXYZABCDEFGHIJKLMNOPQ
K   QRSTUVWXYZABCDEFGHIJKLMNOP
L   PQRSTUVWXYZABCDEFGHIJKLMNO
M   OPQRSTUVWXYZABCDEFGHIJKLMN
N   NOPQRSTUVWXYZABCDEFGHIJKLM
O   MNOPQRSTUVWXYZABCDEFGHIJKL
P   LMNOPQRSTUVWXYZABCDEFGHIJK
Q   KLMNOPQRSTUVWXYZABCDEFGHIJ
R   JKLMNOPQRSTUVWXYZABCDEFGHI
S   IJKLMNOPQRSTUVWXYZABCDEFGH
T   HIJKLMNOPQRSTUVWXYZABCDEFG
U   GHIJKLMNOPQRSTUVWXYZABCDEF
V   FGHIJKLMNOPQRSTUVWXYZABCDE

W   E F G H I J K L M N O P Q R S T U V W X Y Z A B C D
X   D E F G H I J K L M N O P Q R S T U V W X Y Z A B C
Y   C D E F G H I J K L M N O P Q R S T U V W X Y Z A B
Z   B C D E F G H I J K L M N O P Q R S T U V W X Y Z A

With this, we write "LOVE" repeatedly above our plaintext, and use the cipher column corresponding to each letter to encipher our message. The plaintext letter is at the left, and we run across each row until we find the letter under the key word letter. The text "I need you. Come at once" would read:

Keyword: L O V E L O V E L O V E L O V E L O
Plaintext: I N E E D Y O U C O M E A T O N C E
Ciphertext: d b r a i q h k j a j a l v h r j k

The strength of even a four-cipher polyalphabet system is obvious. Here we see two digraphs, "ja," which have entirely different plaintext meanings. The most common letter in English, "E" becomes" "r" "a" and "k."

This type of cipher is much stronger than the simple substitution, but as we'll see in the code-breaking chapter, vulnerable to analysis. A weak point is the use of only four ciphers. Using a longer key word would increase security because it would bring in more individual ciphers. There is another way of using the alphabet table that is perhaps the most secure of all, but its weakness is that one garbled letter can make it impossible for the addressee to decipher the message. This is the "autokey."

THE AUTOKEY CIPHER

This cipher, in its simplest form, requires no key word. The sender and the addressee agree that each message will always begin with a certain letter, for example "A." Another way to decide the key might be to use the first letter of the sender's surname. Yet another way is to use the first letter of the day of the week it is sent. This can cause problems, though, with delayed messages. The addressee will start getting garble and will have to try working backwards until he finds the right letter.

The principle of the autokey is that the cipher letter determines the cipher used for the next letter. Let's work again with the same message as above, and use the alphabet table used with the "LOVE" keyword exercise:

I NEED YOU COME AT ONCE

We'll begin with cipher alphabet "A" to encipher the first letter of the message, which is "I." We go down the left column until we find "I" and take the letter next to it in the first cipher column, to get "S." We use the "S" cipher alphabet to encipher the next letter, "N." This gives us "F." Looking at the top row we find the "F" column, and we find the letter "B" in the same row as the "E" in the extreme left column. Working this way the final result is:

```
I   NEED   YOU   COME   AT   ONCE
S   FBXU   WIO   MYMI   IP   BOMI
```

This short message used twelve cipher alphabets, and only the "B," and "O" got used twice, but for a different letter each time "M" was used three times, twice for the same letter, and there were four "I"s, only twice for the same letter. If we were to rearrange this message into five-letter groups, it would be, for all practical purposes, unbreakable. This may appear hard to believe, but even with the assistance of a super-computer, a message this short, and with no repetitions, is totally secure.

The fatal flaw in the autokey is that, if there is an error in enciphering or transmitting it, the rest of the message is garbage. In deciphering, the addressee looks up the first letter of the ciphertext, "S," in the "A" alphabet, getting "I." He then uses the "S" alphabet to find the next letter's plaintext equivalent, which is "N." Since each letter decipherment depends on the previous one, a single break in the chain makes the rest of the message indecipherable.

The great strength of the autokey is the almost-random enciphering key. With enough messages, however, it's possible to force a solution because there are still only 26 alphabets. It's possible, of course, to construct a cipher table with more than 26 alphabets, but this becomes both clumsy and error-prone in a pencil-and-paper cipher. To get a practically unbreakable pencil-and-paper cipher, we have to go back to numbers.

COORDINATE NUMBER CIPHERS

A more practical number cipher makes use of a grid. We set up a checkerboard with 10 spaces on a side, numbered from "1" to "0." This provides 100 spaces, which we can use to suppress the frequency count of the ciphertext. We do this by including many possible coordinates for the common letters. This was one of the "pocket codes" used by General Leslie R. Groves during the "Manhattan Project" in WWII.[5] Let's see how this looks:

---

[5] *The Code- Breakers*, David Kahn, NY, MacMillan, 1967, p.546

It the coordinate system, we can take the number from the left-hand column as the first digit, and use the one from the top row as the second digit to represent any letter of the alphabet. We have 10 "E"s in 100 spaces, which provides 10 different two-digit numbers to represent it. Using this table, we could encipher "I need you. Come at once." several ways:

	1	2	3	4	5	6	7	8	9	0
1	E	T	A	O	N	R	I	S	H	B
2	C	D	E	F	G	H	I	J	K	L
3	E	T	A	O	N	R	I	S	H	M
4	N	O	P	Q	R	S	T	U	V	W
5	E	T	A	O	N	R	I	S	H	X
6	Y	Z	E	T	A	O	N	R	I	S
7	R	I	S	H	E	T	A	O	I	N
8	E	O	T	A	N	S	H	R	L	U
9	T	D	B	R	E	F	E	E	T	A
0	S	R	H	R	D	L	U	E	T	O

we use usual

1715115122611421423095131254152181
6967236305614221543081334766352195
7255319598610021783075840982412108

Few double-digit combinations repeat. The letter "C" have
only one combination, "21." This cipher can easily hold up a
code-breaker for a few hours, but it's slightly clumsy to use. Let's
try another type of grid, one used by the Soviet Secret Service
during WWII.[6] In this one, we'll use both single and double-digit
numbers:

	0	1	2	3	4	5	6	7	8	9
	E	T	A	O	N	R	I	S	H	
8	C	D	F	G	I	J	K	L	M	
9	P	Q	S	U	V	W	X	Y	Z	B

This cipher doesn't follow the usual practice of starting with
the left column. To encipher, we start along the top row. One
obvious point about the way we've set up this cipher is that the
most common letters in the alphabet, E, T, A, 0, N, R, I, S, H, are
represented by only one digit of ciphertext. Let's see how this
works with our standard message:

1	NEED	YOU	COME	AT	ONCE
6	40018	79339	083880	21	34080

We can see immediately that, while this cipher offers
economy in that the most common letters are single-digit
ciphertext, there- are problems in deciphering. For example, the
combination "08" can mean "C" or "EH." This is an annoyance
which can slow down the addressee's work. Another, and more
serious, problem is that this cipher is still only simple
substitution. A professional code-cracker would eat this for

---

[6] *Ibid*, p. 636.

breakfast. This brings us to the one truly unbreakable cipher
which we can use to disguise the message: the nonrepetitive key.

As we'll see in the chapter on code-breaking, and as we've
suggested here, the weakness of any cipher is in the patterns left
in the enciphered message. A code-breaker can intuitively see
that a two-letter code word can easily be "IT," "IN," "AN," "AT,"
"ON," or "TO." With this, he can guess that any similar
combinations farther on in the message stand for the same
letters. Likewise, when he sees two similar letters or numbers,
such as "88" he may guess that they are doubled vowels or
consonants, again very common in our language. There are few
such combinations, and this again provides an insight into the
hidden meaning.

Even with multiple-alphabet ciphers, there is a recurrence
after a certain amount of ciphertext. A code-breaker can place
texts of two or more messages against each other and note any
repetitions. Once he spots a pattern, he'll have a start at breaking
into the cipher. Only very short messages are proof against code-
cracking. We'll go further into the reasons for this in our
code-breaking section. For the moment, let's note that the only
absolute guarantee against technical code-breaking is an infinite
key. The principle is elementary, and easy to use.

RANDOM NUMBERS

We need a list of random numbers, and we add each number
to a number in the ciphertext, using non-carrying addition. Let's
begin again with the message from above. To this we'll add a set
of numbers generated by a random-number generator included
in a small hand calculator, the CASIO fx-82B. (See Figure 5).

Enciphering one code or cipher text with another is called
"supcrencipherment," and is a common tactic that causes

disproportionate difficulties for the code-breaker. We'll encounter this again in subsequent chapters.

Now we add them, but in a special way for encipherment. This is non-carrying addition, also known as the "Fibonacci System," or "Chinese arithmetic." We add the two numbers, and simply don't carry forward the first digit of any sum greater than 9. This is for brevity, but also because carrying numbers

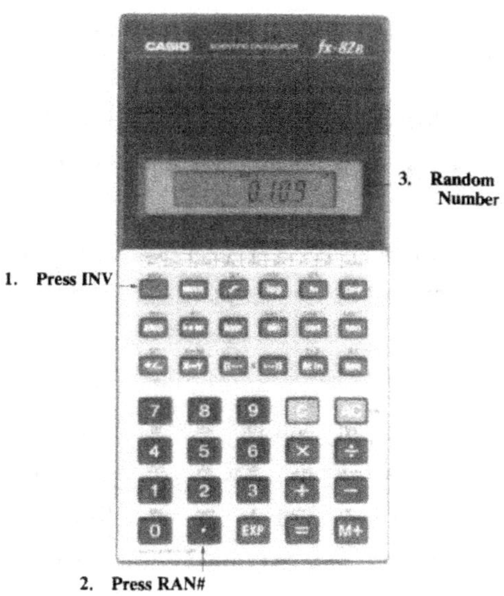

FIGURE 5

To generate a three-digit random number using the Casio fx-82B calculator, first press the INV key in the extreme upper left-hand corner. Then press the decimal key - it has the word RAN# above it (second key from left in the bottom row). A new three-digit random number will be produced each time the process is repeated.

Forward would spoil the random distribution.[7] Here's how this sort of addition looks:

---

[7] *Spy-Catcher*, Peter Wright, NY, Dell Books, 1988, p. 227.

I NEED YOU COME AT ONCE
64001879339083880210408O   ciphertext
58289164507770198145858I   random numbers

1228093383675397835525 61   Superenciphered version

This is our ciphertext, and because random numbers have no
pattern, they have no systematic repetitions. This makes any
effort at breaking the cipher by teasing out patterns futile. The
"22" we see doesn't stand for a repeated letter, but for the "NE"
in the actual message. The repetition "33" stands for "Y." We also
see a "93" and a "39" in the ciphertext, but these don't stand for
reversed letters.

To decipher the message, the addressee needs a copy of the
key. He then subtracts the key from the ciphertext.

122809338)67539783552561
58289164507770198145858I

64001879339083880210408O

The rule for subtraction is the reverse of that used for
addition. If the lower number is larger than the one from which
it's to be subtracted, we assume that the upper number has a "1"
before a. To get the first number, 6, we assume that we're
subtracting 5 from 11.

There are some problems with obtaining random numbers.
We can't simply sit down and write any numbers that come into
our heads. We'll be unconsciously including patterns. A better
choice is to use a book with lots of statistics, such as the World
Almanac. This offers a cheap and commonly-available mass of

random numbers. Because we're only interested in the numbers. we don't need the current edition, and can pick up almanacs from previous years very cheaply in second-hand bookstores. Another commonly-available source is the stock and bond price listings in the financial pages of the newspaper. If the source is a printed one, we may have to include the information in the enciphered message. For example, the first, or tenth number group can be the page number we're using for this message. Let's say we obtained the random numbers for our message from Page 67 of a certain year's almanac. We'd arrange the message as follows:

00067 12280 93383 67539 78355 25610

Breaking the message into five-number groups and adding a null at the end adds to the difficulties the code-breaker will face. Let's note that we can also include the page number at the end of the message, this way:

12280 93383 67539 78355 25610 00067

Another feature of using random numbers is that the five-number groups will also read like code groups. There is no scientific or mathematical way for the code-breaker to determine whether he's working with a code or a cipher, because many codes use random-number groups.

There are ways of generating quick and dirty pseudo-random numbers, but the simplest ones don't offer much security against a skilled and determined code-breaker. One way is to use the current date, repetitively, as the additive. Another is to use either the sender's or the addressee's birthdate. This isn't very good security, and it's possible to enhance it by using the current date and both birthdates in sequence. This is still quick and dirty, however.

A slight upgrade is using a scientific calculator with a random-number function, such as the Casio fx-82B noted above. This costs between ten and fifteen dollars retail. Another model is the Sharp Model #506, in the same price bracket. A yet more complex way of generating random numbers is using a computer program, such as the ones listed in Marotta's Code Book.[8]

None of these are true random-number generators, however. They all use very complex equations with subroutines to put together strings of numbers that don't repeat quickly and which have very subtle patterns. It's only logical to see that any generating system which depends on an equation, however complex, will leave its pattern in the numbers. For most applications, it doesn't matter. Most people cannot dope out a cipher that uses pseudo-random numbers. If there's a good chance that a government will become interested in the contents of your messages, you'll need something more secure if you want your cipher to be totally impenetrable. For this, you need true random numbers. One source is a statistical table of some sort. Another is translating text into numbers, and we'll get into this technique in the chapter on codes.

THE ONE-TIME PAD

This is a way of providing a secret agent with sets of random numbers for field use. One-time pads have been used by the secret services of many nations, although they were invented in

---

[8] *The Code Book*, Third Edition, Michael Marotta, Port Townsend, WA, Loompanics Unlimited, 1987, pp. 21-24

Germany. [9] The reason for the name "one-time" pad is that each sheet on the pad is used once and discarded.

The one-time pad is a set of grids with a number inside each rectangle. There are many rows of numbers that look like this:

2	4	3	7	1	4	7	9	2	5	1	9	5	3	1
3	5	6	3	5	6	8	9	7	2	3	2	4	3	0
1	3	4	5	7	4	8	2	6	2	7	3	9	4	2
0	8	6	5	3	1	2	1	5	6	8	9	8	4	3
1	5	9	2	6	0	1	4	8	0	2	3	6	4	5
4	2	5	3	1	4	5	8	3	6	9	6	7	8	2

Each number comes from a random numbering system, whether true or pseudo-random. However, the odds are that for an agency to go to this trouble, they'll also produce a genuine random number system.

The advantage of the one-time pad is that it's a simple and unbreakable cipher system. In use, the pads are produced in sets of two. The agent takes one pad with him, leaving the other with the "home office." He enciphers his messages, using the sheets in sequence off the top of the pad, and discarding it after one use. The decipherer at the home office follows the same sequence, discarding each sheet after using it because he knows that he'll never get another message using that sheet.

The major disadvantage of the one-time pad is the risk of it being found if one is caught. It's a dead give-away because a one-time pad has no other use. Unlike a book of statistics, or a dictionary, there's no plausible explanation for its possession.

Unlike a key that the agent can keep in his head, there's no way to use a one-time pad except by physically having one. This

---

[9] *The Code-Breakers*, p. 402.

dictates a hiding-place, and any hiding-place is vulnerable to discovery through search or bad luck.

For certain types of high-level diplomatic and military messages, the one-time pad is practical. The pads are secure in protected offices, and the code clerks are not clandestine operatives.

OTHER TECHNIQUES

As we'll see, the substitution cipher is only one type of cipher. In certain cases, another type is more suitable for the task. For extra security, it's also possible to combine two or more different methods. We'll look at different systems to understand these possibilities.

There are also labor-saving devices used in cryptography, usually by government and corporations. These are electro-mechanical systems, and we'll discuss them next.

5

Electro-Mechanical Ciphers

Electro-mechanical systems have dominated the crypto-graphic field during most of the Twentieth Century. However, their roots go back almost two centuries.

As we noted before, Thomas Jefferson devised a cipher-generating "machine" that was very advanced for its day. Although it was based upon the polyalphabetical table, it offered far greater security. The device consisted of 26 wooden discs placed upon a spindle, as shown in Figure 6 on the next page. Each disc had the alphabet evenly spaced around its rim. The letters were in different order on each disc. To use it, the sender rotated the first disc until the first letter of his message was facing him. A ruler helped line up subsequent letters. He then rotated the second disc until the second letter of his message was in line with the first. He repeated this step for the rest of the discs. At that point, the sender had a choice of copying any of the other 25 rows of letters for his ciphertext. With that done, he went on to encipher another row.

To decipher, the addressee had merely to line up his rotors according to the letters in the message, and turn the rotor system until he saw an intelligible line. The device offered polyalphabetic security, but it was also possible to scramble the order of the rotors on the spindle. This was the basis of the U.S. Army Signal Corps' M-94 enciphering device, issued in 1922.[10]

---

[10] *The Code-Breakers*, David Kahn, NY, MacMillan, 1967, p.325

An advantage of the M-94 is that it's simple to use. "Designed by geniuses for use by idiots" is a good description.

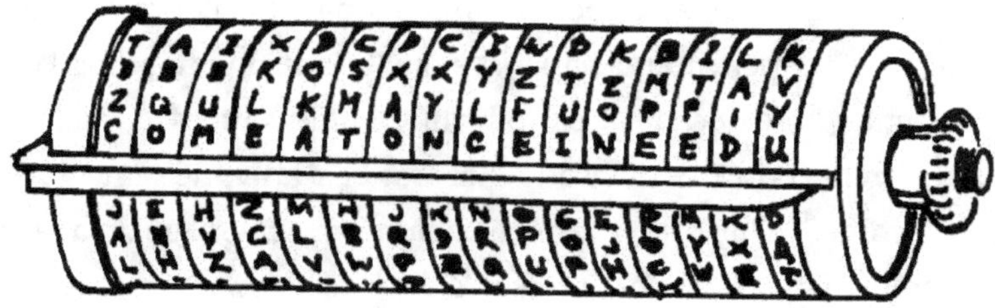

FIGURE 6

Thomas Jefferson was a "founding father" of encryption.
The device shown here is a rotor designed by Jefferson.

POLYALPHABET THEORY

Let's recap the principle of polyalphabet substitution before getting into the complications of million-letter alphabets. We know this using a simple substitution is almost like using no cipher at all, because the cipher letters retain the frequency pattern of the plaintext. Cipher-makers have made huge efforts to suppress these ciphertext frequency patterns, and to suppress any patterns at all. Using more than one alphabet increases the problems for the code-breaker, but he can still detect patterns when the alphabets begin to repeat.

The non-repetitive key, as we've seen, is the perfectly unbreakable enciphering method. The problem with it is that to encipher all of the messages needed requires an unwieldly number of one-times pads or other sources of non-repeating keys. It's not practical to use one-time keys for all messages. There are, however, some workable solutions.

THE ROTOR MACHINES

What if it were possible to use a series of alphabets a couple of hundred thousand alphabets long without repeating? How about a string of alphabets a million long? It isn't practical using any sort of pencil-and-paper system, but during the First World War, and the decade after, four different inventors in four different countries devised what was basically the same machine.[11] This used rotors to encipher the message, in a fashion somewhat like that of Jefferson's device. There was one critical difference which made the ciphers much more secure: The rotors' positions changed after every letter enciphered!

In practice, working an electro-mechanical rotor machine is like typing with an electric typewriter which types a different letter each time we press the same key. We may press "A" a hundred times, and each time a different letter appears, with no order or pattern that we can see.

The way this happens is the heart of the rotor machine. The device uses an electric rotor to re-route the electrical impulses. The rotor is a thick disc with 26 electrical contacts evenly spaced around each face. Within the rotor are wires connecting the contacts on one face to those on the opposite side, so that a circuit will open up between contacts at different positions. The rotor is on a spindle between two other contact plates, each with 26 contacts. The device is wired between a typewriter keyboard and an electric printer. Let's say we press the "A" key. The letter "C" actually prints on the paper. The electrical current also operates a solenoid which flips a tooth into a ratchet, turning the rotor 1/26 of a turn. This lines up the contacts slightly differently. Hitting the "A" key again this time prints an "S," let's say. The solenoid and ratchet turn the disc another increment, and typing

---

[11] *Ibid*, pp. 411-434.

"A" this time prints an "M." What we now have is a
polyalphabetic printer using 26 different alphabets. This is still
not remarkable, although it makes a good labor-saving device
known as an "on-line" encryption machine. This enciphers the
message without any special effort by the operator.

If we add a second rotor to the spindle, between the first and
the contact plate, and a second solenoid and ratchet, we have an
entirely different machine. The second rotor shifts forward one
space only after the first has made a complete tum, when a stud
on its rim trips a switch to actuate the solenoid for the second
rotor. Now, after typing 26 letters, typing "A" again won't give a
"C," but another letter, because the second rotor has re-routed
the current according to its own wiring, which is different from
the first rotor's pattern. This gives us 26 x 26 alphabets, or 676.
This means that the encipherment will not start repeating until
after 676 letters. A third rotor, which start<; turning only after
the first two have completed their cycles, brings the interval up
to 17,576. Adding a fourth gives us almost half a million
alphabets, and using five gives us over 11 million.

Let's look at a patent office diagram of a cipher rotor machine
(Figure 7).

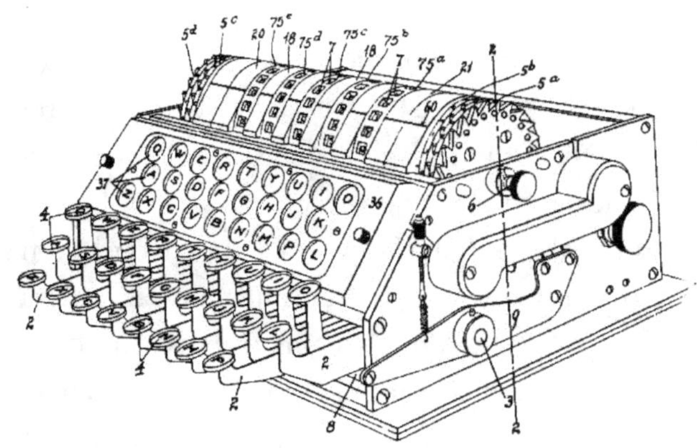

FIGURE 7

Edward Hebern's "Electric Code Machine

We can see that the original idea of this early model was not on-line encryption, but simply enciphering. Hitting a key only lit a bulb behind a letter on the board. The ratchets are mechanically operated, and this device will run on battery power. This makes it suitable for military field use.

Let's inspect the works of the famous "Enigma" machine (Figure 8).

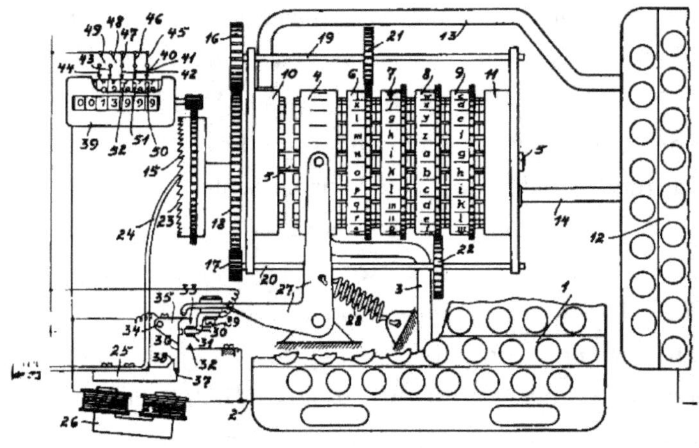

FIGURE 8

Arthur Scherbius "Enigma" enciphering rotor.

We see how a lever turns the ratchet manually for each letter encipherment. We also see how it's possible to set the rotor individually for each message. A diagram at the upper left shows a schematic for wiring a rotor.

Incredibly, this isn't the last word, either in operation or the degree of security possible. To transmit a message, it's necessary for both the sending and receiving machine to start at the same point, with rotors in both machines in the same positions. This means that there must be a "key," to allow setting the rotors with the key letters next to a reference mark. The key can change

50

every month, week, or day. During the latter part of the war, the Germans changed the key every eight hours.

Various models of these machines were available on the open market during the 1920s. The military market was poor, and the inventors' only opportunities of making enough sales lay in the corporate world. With machines openly available, security had to depend on the keys, which users kept secret.

Another choice was having spare discs, all wired differently. In certain cases, it was possible to procure discs on special order, with wiring patterns different from all other discs manufactured. This meant that, even with the keys and a similar machine, an unauthorized person could not read the ciphers unless he managed to obtain one of the special rotors as well.

There were also spare rotors available. This allowed even more complexity. With a five-rotor machine and five spares, there were 25 different combinations available even before starting with the keys. Knowing the cipher key wouldn't help without also having the rotor key.

A mechanical improvement was the "reflector," which was a special contact plate at the end of the machine. Instead of taking off the current at the contact to feed it to a typewriter key, a wire would route it to another contact on the plate, to send it back through the rotors. Final take-off would be at the starting position, with the current having passed through the system of rotors twice. This gave the effect of ten rotors.

The plug-board, located between the keyboard and the rotor system, was another wrinkle. There were wires and plugs that the operator could arrange according to different patterns, or keys. This changed the order in which the impulses started through the rotor system. Thus, the impulses went from the keyboard through the plug-board, on through the rotor circuits, and finally to the printer (Figure 9).

The plug-board was redundant. While it offered greater security, it was unnecessarily complex to operate. At least as much security would have been available with far less trouble by adding another rotor.

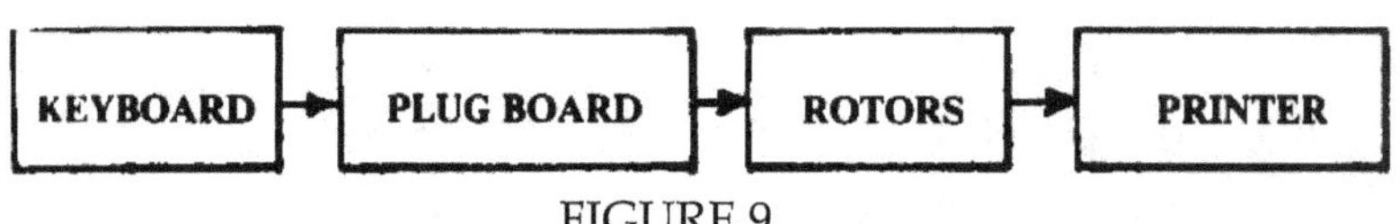

KEYBOARD → PLUG BOARD → ROTORS → PRINTER

FIGURE 9

Schematic of electric rotor cipher machine.

The Enigma machine had two interesting features: reciprocity and exclusivity. The reciprocal feature meant that the machine would work exactly backward if required. Typing in an "A" ' gave a "D," for example, but typing a "D" would give an "A." This made deciphering easier. Exclusivity meant that the Enigma W(mid never give the same letter as ciphertext for itself. Typing an "A" would never produce an "A."

Unfortunately, these features did not give extra security. The 1·xdusivity feature limited the choices by 1/26 each time, and this made it easier for the code-breaker. The reciprocity feature made it easier for a poorly-trained operator to use.

The first generation of cipher machines were primitive, offering good security but poor convenience. The Enigma at first required two operators, one to read the message and a second to work the machine. The enciphered message then had to go to the communications room for transmission through regular channels. A later development was "on-line" encipherment. This simplifies the task for the operator, who types the message while the machine enciphers and transmits it simultaneously. The advantages are increased speed and convenience, and reduced errors.

SOLID-STATE MACHINES

The electro-mechanical machine is obsolete. Developments in integrated circuits and solid-state logic chips provide the opportunities for building all-electronic machines such as the "Cryptel," which is about the size of a portable electric typewriter and contains a "modem" to transmit messages over telephone lines.

SELF-DESTRUCT

Capture of a modern cipher machine can be a national disaster, which is why governments take extreme steps to prevent it. Normally, these machines are in use only at heavily secured locations. In foreign embassies, they're always behind locked doors at the interior of the building. There are enough walls and doors to delay an intruder long enough for the machines to be destroyed.

The armed forces try to keep their cryptographic facilities in secure locations. On navy ships, the cipher room is always deeply buried inside the ship, behind a locked door. Traditionally, ships' captains were under orders to throw the code books over- board if surrender was unavoidable. Today, this is unlikely, and the code room contains enough devices to destroy its contents in case of capture. Sometimes, this doesn't work very well, as in the case of the U.S.S. Pueblo.

The army tries to keep cipher facilities far enough behind the lines to be relatively safe. Still, there's the possibility of a surprise attack, or a landing by paratroopers, and these facilities have their own "bodyguards." Cipher clerks are required to be armed, and one or more remains on duty 24 hours a day.

All machines are equipped with self-destruction devices, usually consisting of an incendiary bomb within the "guts" of the machine. Pulling a red knob attached to a cord or wire drags a piece of magnesium through an abrasive igniter, and this sets off the "thermite" mixture. The heat generated is enough to melt down the vital components within a few seconds. Because thermite carries its own oxygen, it can't be put out with a fire extinguisher. Cipher machine operators are under standing orders to destroy the machine before retreating, even at the risk of their lives.

SCRAMBLERS

These are devices to make the human voice unintelligible to eavesdroppers. Scramblers in various forms have been in service for many decades. Indeed, a primitive scrambler was patented in 1881.[12] This primitive device chopped the conversation into short fragments and routed them alternately over two different lines..

Frequency inversion was the next step, and several commercial devices appeared during the 1920s. These simply invert the frequencies of human speech, making the low frequencies come out high and vice versa. This gives the speech a whining, squealing quality which is harder to understand than unaltered speech.

Band-splitting was the basis of the Bell System "A-3," devised during the 1930s. This broke the speech up into bands, switched 1heir frequencies, inverted them, and when used in conjunction with a radio-telephone, switched transmission frequencies every several seconds to make eavesdropping harder.

---

[12] *Ibid*, pp. 411-434.

Although digital sound recording is commonly-available
technology today, an early application, a couple of decades ago,
was for voice privacy. Breaking speech up into digital "bits"
allows enciphering in a way that's absolutely unintelligible to
anyone without digital equipment and the cipher key.[13] This was
originally called "PCM," or Pulse Code Modulation, and it lends
itself to rapid encipherment by a one-time or a pseudo-random
generator. This technique is pretty well established now. It's
been advertised in technical and military magazines for a couple
of decades.

---

[13] *Ibid*, pp. 711-712

6

Transposition Ciphers

The other major type of cipher is the transposition cipher. In this, there are one or more ways of mixing up the order of the letters to make the message unreadable. Let's look at a few sample transposition ciphers quickly, before getting on to the professional-grade ciphers.

THE RECTANGLE

One of the simplest ways of enciphering a short message is to write it in several lines:

```
C O M E A T
O N C E I N
E E D Y O U
R I G H T N
O W X X X X
```

We then re-write the message by rows:
COERO ONEIW MCDGX EEYHX AIOTX TNUNX
This appears quite unintelligible, but the simplicity of the system makes it unlikely to hold up a code-breaker very long. This also makes it easy for the sender to encipher his message. There's no complicated key to memorize.

A problem with this type of cipher is that capacity is limited. We could choose a larger rectangle, such as one with 48 places.

This factors out to 6 x 8 or 4 x 12. The message doesn't have to come exactly to 48 letters, as we can fill empty spaces with nulls. The largest practical size is 72 places. This factors out to 10 combinations.

There's no reason why more than one rectangle can't be used if the message is longer than the capacity of one. For simplicity, it's just as easy to use two 36-letter patterns as it is to make one large 72-letter one. There's actually no advantage to one or the other regarding security.

THE RAIL FENCE CIPHER

FIGURE 10

Using the rail fence cipher,
a message is divided and rewritten

In this simple system, we write the message horizontally, in several long rows, as shown in Figure 10. Once we've divided the message into segments with diagonal slashes, we re-write it, starting from the extreme bottom left:

AOTYR ECORF OUOOM RWREI WMAGI ETHLX
OTLXN ABXCW EXEAT XIYOX NTOXE OLEMD

Deciphering involves arranging the letters in diagonals.[14]

GRILLS

A grill is a template, a piece of paper or cardboard with squares or rectangular slots designed to fit over a standard sheet of paper. The sender writes his message in the slots, removes the grill, and fills in the rest of the sheet, constructing words as best he can. A more ingenious grill is called the "Cardano Grill," after the Italian who invented it. This is a rotating grill with 36 places, only nine of which are cut out. It is shown in Figure 11.

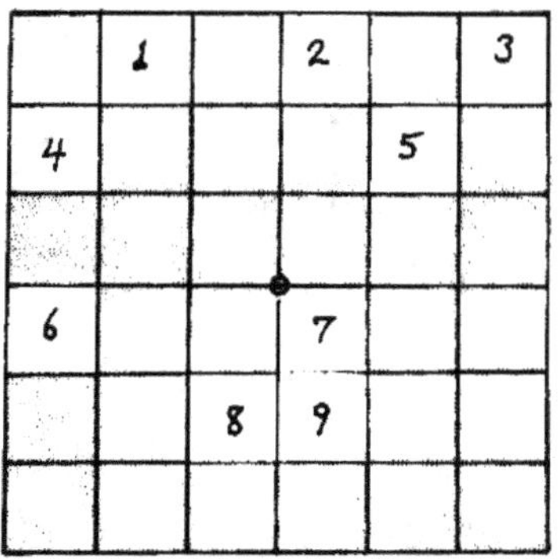

FIGURE 11

The Cardano Grill

Note that this grill has a pivot hole in the center. The sender begins his message following the numbered holes, then rotates the grill 90 degrees, using a pin through the pivot hole. The cutouts now are lined up on nine fresh places on the paper,

---

[14] The Code Book, Third Edition, Michael E. Marotta, Port Townsend, WA, Loompanics Unlimited, 1987, p. 7

allowing another nine letters. Now the writer rotates the grill again, writes another nine letters, and repeats the cycle.[15]

This sort of cipher provides more security than a geometric one for short messages. It doesn't take much time or ingenuity to take a message of 25 or 36 letters and to try it in several arrangements. Arranging the letters in a square or rectangle allows reading up or down, backwards, forward, and diagonally. The Cardano Grill, while not impenetrable, is harder to dope out.

ADFGX

At times it's possible to gain good security by combining a simple substitution with a simple transposition cipher. One of the most successful was "ADFGX," the German WWI cipher The substitution cipher turns letters into digraphs, using a grid and only five cipher letters:

	a	d	f	g	x
a	C	Y	U	M	V
d	D	J	F	S	N
f	B	Q	R	L	W
g	G	E	H	O	A
x	P	Z	K	X	T

Having only 25 spaces meant that it was necessary to drop one letter. In this case, "I" is missing, with "J" taking its place when necessary. To encipher, we find the letter in the grid, and start with the cipher letter at the left, then the one at the top, for

---

[15] *Secret Warfare: The Battle of Codes and Ciphers*, Brim Norman, NY, Dorset Press, 1973, pp. 20-24.

the digraph. "Y" becomes "ad." Now let's encipher our usual message:

I	NEED	YOU	COME	AT	ONE
dd	dxgdgdda	adggaf	aaggaggd	gxxx	ggdxaagd

The next step is to write the message itself in grid form, and to number each column according to a memorized key:[16]

1	9	8	7	4	6	3	5	2	0
d	d	d	x	g	d	g	d	d	a
a	d	d	d	a	f	a	a	g	g
a	g	g	g	g	X	X	X	g	g
d	x	a	a	g	d				

The "0" stands for "10." We then take each column in numerical order to write out the message:

daadd gggax gaggd axdfx dxgda dggad dgxag g

One problem with this cipher is that the last group consists of only one letter. Adding nulls consisting of letters such as "adfgx" would confuse the addressee because they'd interfere with the transposition order in the deciphering. Using other letters would stand out and tell a code-breaker exactly which letters were nulls.

The Germans later brought out a second-generation mixed cipher "ADFGVX." This built upon a grid of 36 characters, and included numbers:

	a	d	f	g	v	x
a	C	1	5	U	M	V

---

16 *Ibid.*, pp. 63-71.

	D	J	F	2	S	N
d	D	J	F	2	S	N
f	B	9	R	L	3	W
g	4	G	E	8	O	A
v	T	Y	7	H	Q	0
x	P	Z	K	X	6	1

Note that this restores the letter "I," as well as adding the digits "1-0."

"ADFGVX" was a very successful field cipher because it was truly hard to crack. The French cryptanalysts never broke more than a few keys, and these only during heavy traffic days.[17]

"ADFGVX" was vulnerable, however. The problems with a were that the Germans sent identical messages to different headquarters, and that the digraphs gave frequency counts that were definitely monoalphabetic.

---

[17] *The Code-Breakers*, David Kahn, NY, MacMillan, 1967, ц 344.

7

Codes

A "code," as we've seen, is a crypto-system in which we replace entire words or phrases with code words, groups, or numbers. Because there's no statistical relationship between cleartext words and phrases and their code equivalents, breaking a code is much harder. Also, because there's no internal consistency between letter and number groups, and no logical progressions, a code-breaker who obtains a coded message and its cleartext together doesn't have a lever to pry loose the rest of the code.

Let's look at the various types of codes, their make-up, and different applications.

MILITARY CODE NAMES

Military services maintain lists of code words to assign to specific military operations, placenames, and equipment. A typical list of military code words contains terms such as these:

AMBER	MOUNTAIN
BAKER	NEBULA
CHARLIE	ORANGE
DELTA	PRESTO
EGGPLANT	ROBERTS
FIREFLY	SHOTGUN
GIANT	TAILOR
GOLD	URANUS

HORNET   VOTER
INTACT   YELLOW
JERSEY   ZERO

Code words of this sort may be nouns, verbs, adjectives or anything else, as long as they don't suggest what they represent Lists of code words not yet chosen go to various military commands, with care not to duplicate code words between lists. Commanders choose code words to denote various plans, projects, and objectives, and discard the code word once the operation is over.

COMMERCIAL CODES

These were originally called "telegraph codes," because they were devised to save transmission time and costs for their users. The first of these came about in the late Eighteenth Century when a commercial semaphore system made its debut in France.[18] With the invention of the telegraph, many other codes appeared. The main design points for compilers of commercial codes were to minimize errors by not making the code words too similar and open to confusion, and to pack as much meaning as possible into a single word.

Dictionary words were liable to misspelling if the telegrapher dropped a single dot or dash, and code compilers compensated for this by creating artificial code words, groups of syllables with no other meaning. These were designed only for error-free transmission. [19]

LETTERS OR NUMBERS

---

[18] *The Code-Breakers*, David Kahn, NY, MacMillan, 1967, p. 836.
[19] *Ibid.*, pp. 839-842.

In designing a code, the basic question is whether code words shall be letters or digits. Letters have the advantage that they can form pronounceable words, for verbal transmission. Numbers, on the other hand, lend themselves very well to "super-encipherment." This means enciphering the code groups for extra security.

Whether one or the other, custom is to list code groups of five characters, with their meanings, in two sections. The first is for encoding and lists the meanings alphabetically. The decoding section lists the code groups in order.

Why five characters? With all of the permutations possible with 26 letters in the alphabet, about eleven million combinations are possible. With only ten digits possible, 1 through 0, we're down to 100,000 combinations, but these will still cover more than enough for most purposes.

THE DICTIONARY CODE

A simple way of constructing a code for general use is to seek the words in a pocket dictionary and write the number of the page, and the number of the word on the page. This results in a five-digit group.

Page 1 would register as "001," Page 2 would be "002," etc. Few, if any, pocket dictionaries have more than 999 pages, so three digits suffice. Likewise, few pocket dictionaries have more than 99 words on a page.

A pocket dictionary is desirable because, for our purposes, we only need the listing of the word. A detailed definition, with etymology, etc., is unnecessary and takes up space.

There's one problem with using a dictionary code. Certain common words, such as THE, AND, AN, IT, TO, etc., will repeat often, always with the same code group. One way to solve this problem is to use a second paperback book to supplement the dictionary. The second book may be a novel or non-fiction. Whatever the subject, it's likely to have words in their normal distribution in the language. These will serve as "spares" for encoding to foil a code-breaker. Whenever a common word turns up, we find it in the spare book and write the page and word number. To differentiate between the two books, we use a five-digit number for the dictionary and a six digit one for the spare book. We'll need the extra digit because there are usually more than 99 words on a page in a novel or non-fiction book. Because they're common words, we'll have no trouble finding them when we need them.

An observant code-breaker might guess that, because some code groups begin with one or more zeros, they refer to pages, and he might guess that this is a dictionary code. The way to counter that, super-encipherment, also adds extra security. A quick and dirty way to do it is to add today's date to each number.

Let's say that today's date is October 6, 1988. We write it as 10/6/88 and add 10688 to each five-digit group. If the group has six digits, we use a zero before the 6: 10/06/88, and add 100688, using non-carrying addition. The weakness here is that the same super-encipherment goes on in every group. If the code-cracker can dope out one or two groups, and realize that a date is the super-encipherment, he'll be able to strip it off every group. Once into the code, he'll progressively be able to figure out the meanings of more groups. Worse, he'll realize that the superencipherment is based on a date, and this will give him a head start with future messages.

A better way is adding a list of random numbers to each digit in the code groups. This will disguise the occurrence of zeros and make it doubly difficult to make progress on unlocking the code, even if a lucky event allows the code-cracker to break into the code. Even if he obtains an entire message in clear, he won't know what all the other groups mean because of the random number super-encipherment.

A convenient way to obtain random numbers is to use the pages of the second book. Converting the letters to their alphabetical numbers will provide a long list of digits for super-encipherment. A=1, B=2, etc. It's also possible to number the letters backwards, for slight extra security.[20] There must, however, be a system to advise the addressee on which page to begin. The simplest is to use pages in sequence, omitting title pages within the book. Another is to begin each message with a code group that gives the page number, such as "00015."

When super-enciphering, it's important not to repeat the random numbers. A code-breaker who notices that the first groups of several different messages are the same may decide to stack them in columns and start subtracting each group from the others in the same column, which will reveal factors they have in common. This can provide an entry into the actual code groups.[21]

DISGUISING THE CODE

The logical assumption, when confronted with five-letter groups, is that if they're code groups, they'll be random letters. A frequency count will show a random pattern. One way of causing a code-breaker grief is to use code groups that show a

---

[20] *Secret Warfare: The Battle of Codes and Ciphers*, Bruce Norman, NY, Dorset Press, 1973, pp. 146-147

[21] *The Code-Breakers*, pp. 441-443.

normal or near-normal frequency count. This may sucker him
into trying various transposition permutations.

Another way is to use a frequency distribution, but on the
wrong letters. Instead of using "E" as the most common, we can
use "Z," for example.

THE HOME COMPUTER

We won't spend much time on this, as not everyone has a
home computer. We'll also have to be very general, because the
various computer programs operate with different commands.
Creating a code book quickly and economically with a home
computer requires a database program and a word processing
program. The steps are:

Bring the word processing program's spelling checker
dictionary into an open file. Edit it, deleting unnecessary words.
and adding needed phrases. Store this.

Start another file with the word processing program, and
"read" the list of words into it. Generate a random list of code
groups, numbers or letters, placing them before the dictionary
words and phrases. This will be the encoding part. Print this out.
The only inconvenience in using this part will be that the second
column, containing the meanings, will be alphabetized instead of
the first.

Copy this file and use the "sort" function of the database
program to re-arrange the code groups in order. This will then
be the decoding part. Print this out.

SECURITY

Codes offer the best security. Because they deal with
message, elements that are much harder to tabulate statistically,

normal methods of cryptanalysis don't work well with them. Adding a super-encipherment creates a tangle so dense that most often the code-cracker's only hope is to steal the code.

8

Code-Breaking

This is a difficult subject to follow, because it's deeply buried in secrecy. While we see much material published about techniques of code-making, the other process, code-breaking, is a almost ignored. There are a few books written by amateur cryptanalysts, such as Gaines,[22] and a few others dealing with war-time code-cracking. The Gaines book is for code and cipher hobbyists. The others are about real-life, heavy duty code cracking. One such is *The Broken Seal,* by Ladislas Farago.[23] This deals with the cracking of the Japanese diplomatic code, which gave a last-minute warning of the Pearl Harbor attack. Another is *The Ultra Secret*, which gives a sketchy account of how the British made use of Enigma intercepts.[24] Most of these hooks appeared decades after the events they describe, and were heavily censored.

There's a reason for this, of course. Those with experience in government code-breaking are usually enjoined from publicizing anything about their work. The little that comes out is heavily censored to avoid giving an actual or potential enemy clues about current efforts and capabilities. An example is the revelation of the "bombe," the British code-breaking computer of

---

[22] *Cryptanalysis,* Helen Gaines, NY, Dover Books, 1956

[23] *The Broken Seal,* Ladislas Farago, NY, Random House, 1967.

[24] *The Ultra Secret,* Frederick Wintherbotham, London, Futura, 1975.

the early 1940s. This machine, which they inherited from Polish code-breakers, was long obsolete before British authorities allowed a public word to appear.

Cryptanalysis, or code-breaking, is usually the most secret of all government activities. It's more closely held than the codes the government uses. Governments admit they use codes and ciphers for their military and diplomatic traffic, and only classify technical information about the systems themselves.

However, all governments deny even attempting to read other nations' encrypted traffic. Any sort of eavesdropping is almost always a deep and dark secret. There's a very clear and obvious reason for this. A government which can read another's "mail" has a superb advantage in planning, negotiation, and overall competition. Knowing what an enemy, rival, or ally is thinking and planning provides an edge which can quickly disappear once the rival government becomes aware that its communications aren't secure. This is why NSA, the National Security Agency, stays out of the public eye most of the time.

Most of the NSA's activity is aimed at decrypting other nations' communications, and NSA officials apparently feel that the less said about this, the better. This attitude isn't unusual. No nation admits publicly that it reads the codes of other nations with which it is not at war.

Nations spy upon all three: enemies, rivals, and allies. The reason for spying upon an enemy is obvious. A rival may be an economic rival, and knowing future trade plans enables making counter-moves to secure a trade advantage. Reading an ally's communications helps determine if the ally is operating in good faith. One of the nightmares that belligerents have in any alliance is that one or more members will break away and sign a separate peace, as Italy did from Germany in 1943. Warring powers will make almost any concession to keep an ally in the fight, as the

United States did to keep the Soviets fighting during World War II.

Naturally, revealing that one spies upon an ally promotes distrust, which is why this is always undercover. When William Hamilton Martin and Bernon Ferguson Mitchell, two National Security Agency employees, defected to Soviet Russia in 1960, they revealed that their employer was reading the codes of our allies. This caused extreme embarrassment for the United States, which is why the Soviets were eager for Martin and Mitchell to tell all at a press conference.

This secretiveness makes more difficult the task of separating fact from fiction. On one hand, we have seen a rash of books on the theme of "How I Won The War By Code-breaking." These tell how the hero saved his country untold hardship by his force of intellect, relentlessly struggling to tease apart the secrets of the enemy's crypto-system. On the other hand, we see accounts such as the one by General Cesare Ame, head of Italian Military Intelligence during WWII. He relates how his agents stole the American "Black" code from the American Embassy in Rome, and with this his office and the Germans were able to read messages sent by the American military attache in Cairo, Colonel Bonner Fellers. The Italians were able to obtain the American Black Code undetected because two embassy employees were Italian nationals in the pay of the secret service.[25]

Colonel Fellers was no ordinary military attache. He loved his job, and he passed on to his headquarters in Washington every detail he could pick up regarding British military dispositions and plans in the Western Desert. The intercepts gave the Italians vital information about British moves. They passed on the

---

[25] *Secret Warfare: The Battle of Codes and Ciphers*, Bruce Norman, NY, Dorset Press, 1973, pp. 123-131.

messages to their German allies, but did not hand over the entire purloined code. The alliance was not very solid, and there was mutual distrust and rivalry.

The Germans, with some decoded messages in hand courtesy of their Italian allies, had a head start at breaking into the "Black" Code. Black was a regular code with a "super-encipherment" added. The cipher clerk added a fixed number to each code group, and this made it harder to break the code. The key number changed regularly, probably daily, and this avoided giving an eavesdropper a large enough sample of groups to get a break mathematically. However, the Germans had noted that the messages always began with the same salutation codegroup, and this allowed them to find the key number at the outset, and use it to unlock the rest of the message.

Probably every secret service in the world has experts at breaking and entering. This is known, in American slang, as a "black bag job." In Italy, the Carabinieri oversaw these activities. The Carabinieri is the national police, roughly equivalent to the American FBI, which also does black bag jobs. In Britain, the "Security Service" carries out breaking and entering, and warrantless searches.[26]

---

[26] *Spy-Catcher*, Peter Wright, NY, Dell Books, 1988, p. 40. A good part of this book relates how British security agents spied upon Britain's allies, enemies, and neutrals. Between pp. 103-109 we find an account of how British security agents and post office technicians placed an infinity microphone in a telephone in the code room of the Egyptian Embassy. This picked up the sounds of the clerk resetting the rotors of the cipher machine each morning, enabling British code-crackers to read immediately all embassy code traffic. Wright also tells how MI-5 bugged the French Embassy to pick up the settings on their cipher machine.

Purloining codes is a highly specialized skill. More important than obtaining the code is doing it quietly, without detection. If the burglary victim discovers that his code's no longer secure, he'll change it, negating the entire effort. One attempt involved "bugging" the Soviet Embassy in Ottawa. In this case, agents of the Royal Canadian Mounted Police and Britain's MI-5 installed microphones in various rooms, but the Russians apparently knew of the bugging and moved their secret activities to another part of the building.[27]

There's another effect of code-breaking, of interest mainly to propagandists and historians. During WWII, many highly acclaimed military leaders owed their successes to code breaking, which revealed to them the enemy's plans. Germany's General Rommel did so well with his Afrika Korps because he knew the British moves in advance. The American General George Patton had regular transcripts of important German messages to help him in his ·planning. Reputations that seemed so bright become duller in the light of new information.

SKILL OR LUCK?

Amateur code-makers sometimes devise codes or ciphers they think are unbreakable, but are surprisingly easy to crack. However, a reasonably competent cryptographer can devise a code or cipher that will resist analysis for months or years. As

---

[27] *Ibid.*, pp. 78-82. A worse bungle occurred in Portugal in 1943, when two American agents broke into the Japanese Embassy to photograph their cryptographic materials. They did not know that the Japanese diplomatic cipher had already been broken. The agents left traces of their entry, and the Japanese took warning and changed their cryptosystem. *The Hidden World*, R. A. Haldane, New York, Saint Martin's Press, 1976.

we've already seen, various crypto-systems of the major powers remained secure until an enemy obtained a copy of the code or the enciphering machine.

No doubt, there were brilliant code-crackers, but often a certain amount of luck figured into it. Often, a code-breaker obtains an edge which provides an insight into how the code or cipher works, and a key to unraveling it. Breaking into a competently devised crypto-system is so difficult, and takes so much time, that governments make serious efforts to find short-cuts, such as stealing other nations' crypto-systems. Not all are lucky enough to have a code book delivered into their hands by the black bag squad, but sometimes a lucky accident brings it to them.

In 1914 the German cruiser Magdeburg sank after an engagement with Russian ships, and the Russians obtained its code hooks. Unsure of what to do with them, the Russians passed the precious books to their British allies, who knew exactly what to do with them. As Germany's chief naval rival, the Royal Navy had a burning interest in cracking German codes and ciphers, and capture of the German code books gave the code-breaking 1iffice a flying start.

Breaking into the new German electro-mechanical crypto-system, the Enigma, was not as difficult as some authors made it out to be. It wasn't a matter of discovering a pattern in a totally unfamiliar system of digits. Allied code-crackers had a "crib." Actually, the rotor cipher machine had been invented in three different countries by four different men between 1915-1925, and there were commercial versions commonly available. The German military models were more complex, but Allied code-breakers had their vital lead provided by the commercial models purchased over-the-counter. In another case, a German sold secrets of the Enigma to French Intelligence. Once aware of the basic layout, it was logical to deduce the improvements which would make the machine cipher more secure. From this, securing the keys, which often changed daily, was another problem which the code-crackers solved in a short time.

In May, 1941, the British captured a German submarine, the U-110. The crew failed to throw the code books and the Enigma machine overboard, and this gave British cryptanalysts a clear view at the German naval code because they now had the keys for the next several months.[28] Previously, British naval units had captured the extra rotors and the current keys from a disabled German submarine, but this wasn't enough to give them the entire system on a plate.

Defectors sometimes bring tangible help for the code-breakers. When cipher clerk Igor Gouzenko defected from the Soviet Embassy in Ottawa in 1945, he brought with him a batch of secret telegrams as his "admission ticket."[29] These messages not only provided vital information for Western intelligence agencies but allowed a comparison between encoded versions and cleartext. This is a vital step in code-cracking, and enabled reading Soviet coded traffic for several years back.

––––––––––––––––––––

[28] *Top Secret Ultra*, Peter Calvocoressi, NY, Pantheon Books, 1980, p. 86. Earlier that year, a British Commando raid on the Lofoten Islands, off Norway, produced some spare Enigma rotors. The previous year, on October 18,1940, the Italian submarine DURBO surrendered after a depth charging, and the British destroyer H.M.S. Wrestler captured the Italian naval codes. *The Death of the U-Boat*. Edwin P. Hoyt, NY, McGraw-Hill, 1988, pp. 81-83. In March, 1944, an American escort carrier group captured the German U-505 and her Enigma machine off the Azores. *U Boats Under the Swastika*, J.P. Mallmann Showell, NY, Arco Publishing Company, 1974, pp. 70-71.

[29] *The FBI-KGB War*, Robert J. Lamphere, NY, Berkley Books, 1987, pp. 33-35.

Another instance of code-cracking that was top-secret for forty years was that involving the "Finnish code book." During WWII, the Finnish military had captured a Soviet code book that had been partly burned. The American OSS had managed to acquire a good part of this through some sub-rosa transactions with the Finns. A bizarre sequel to this event was that the Secretary of State, Edward Stetinius, protested to President Roosevelt that reading our allies' codes was dirty pool. The President ordered the OSS to return the material to the Soviets. It's almost certain that, before handing it over, OSS officers photostated it. We don't find any admission of this in the source material, though.[30] The author admits that there are certain aspects of the affair that the National Security Agency has

---

[30] *Ibid,* p. 86. Peter Wright, in *Spy-Catcher,* describes this operation in more detail, emphasizing the British end of it He calls it the "greatest Counterintelligence secret in the Western world." The British code name for it was VEN ONA, and its origins involved both the Finnish code book and the Soviet lapse in having some of their agents use them one-time pads more than once. Early in WWII, the Soviets were very short of cipher material, and allowed several uses of the one-time pads to handle the increased secret traffic load. In pp. 227-240, Wright relates how an American cryptanalyst, Meredith Gardner, made the first breaks into the code, and how a massive effort over forty years teased fragments of messages out of the Soviet traffic, which had been recorded by various counterespionage agencies.

Despite the use of advanced computers, and electronic cross-matching of code groups, according to Wright, fewer than 1% of the 200,000 messages recorded yielded anything. In most of the ones in which cryptanalysts gained entry, they got only a few words. This gives a realistic idea of the tremendous difficulties involved in breaking into an enciphered code, even when the enemy blunders.

insisted remain secret to this day.[31] What has come to light, however, is that these decoded messages led to the uncovering of Burgess and Maclean, Harry Gold, and the Rosenbergs. We can also infer that information obtained from Igor Gouzenko helped in the effort, because Soviet officials under diplomatic cover in Canada had a very hot espionage operation running during the Second World War. In keeping with a well-known practice of running an espionage operation from a neighboring country, Soviet spymasters seeking American nuclear bomb secrets operated in both Canada and Mexico.

CRIBS AND PATTERNS

There are many ways in which a code-cracker can make a start in breaking into a crypto-system. Let's consider the cribs first, as these often provide the breakthrough that a technician needs.

Many messages contain stereotyped language, such as addresses, salutations, boilerplate wording, etc. A code-cracker, who knows the forms that the target messages take, can dope out that the first few code groups stand for certain meanings and names. For example, a message sent in the military top-secret cipher may start with:

PRIORITY ONE
ATT: FIRST ARMY HEADQUARTERS
COMMANDING OFFICER
EYES ONLY

---

[31] *Ibid.*, p. 81.

If these lines begin every message, they provide an entry into the crypto-system. Today's code clerks are sophisticated and know how to defeat this. A good way is to break the message in half, and put the second half first. This avoids stereotyped beginnings. The decoding clerk can put the message in order after decrypting.

Another clue is the use of place-names and other proper nouns. If, for example, a diplomatic conference deals with Alsace-Lorraine, it's a simple deduction that the place-name will be somewhere in the text. So will the names of towns and geographic features in the area in question. Names of delegates may also form part of the message. Military traffic contains many place-names during active operations, and these serve as cribs for the code-breaker. This is why a cryptanalyst will always want to know the context of a message before starting his work.

Another crib is the known message. If the Secretary of State hands a foreign ambassador a message to transmit to his government, code-crackers can expect that the embassy will be transmitting it very soon. With cleartext, they can pry the code loose. Again, sophisticated code clerks know how to counter this. They paraphrase the message before encoding it, to prevent a direct cleartext-ciphertext comparison.

A variation on the theme of the known message is the forced message. During the months after Pearl Harbor, American navy cryptanalysts were reading the Japanese naval code, JN-25. They understood enough of the code to make out that the Japanese were planning an important operation in the near future. However, this code also included some code notations within it, obviously for brevity. One was the designation "AF," the place against which the forthcoming operation would take place. American code-crackers were unsure of its meaning, but suspected that it meant "Midway." To confirm this, they "planted" a piece of disinformation, sending a message in a low-grade cipher that Midway Island was short of water. They knew that the Japanese code-crackers could read this cipher, and waited for the reaction. Soon a Japanese message stated that "AF" was short of water.[32]

Sometimes sheer dumb luck provides a way in. A clerk transmits a message in the high-security code or cipher, and receives a reply that the equipment at the receiving end is temporarily out of service. The clerk then sends the same message in another cipher. This provides an entry into both for the codebreaker.

The technique of operation sometimes carries with it a way in for the enemy code-breaker. Rotor machine ciphers, for example, require keys for the initial rotor settings. These are often compiled and issued to field units' months in advance of their use. Warships, for example, need keys for every day they're at sea, and must carry them aboard. Another weakness is that some rotor machines also use a separate key for each message, as well as the day's key. Common practice is to provide this key at the beginning of the message, repeating it to be sure that the recipient gets it. An eavesdropper who understands this gains a head start in breaking into the machine cipher.

For tight security, it's common to change the keys every day. This means that there are very many keys in circulation. The more keys there are, the less dissimilar they can be. Sometimes, after a crypto-system's been in use for several years, we may find some keys only a few positions apart. With so many keys, some messages will overlap, giving access with mathematical analysis.

In other cases, the system brings with it the prospect of human error. A cipher clerk may send a message in the previous

---

[32] *Secret Warfare*, pp. 134-135.

day's key, then catch his error and repeat it with the current key. This provides the code-breaker with a good opening. In other instances, different units will get the same orders, with only the addresses and salutations different. Both cases provide the code-breaker with the same plaintext, and comparing the two messages can give a quick insight into the encryption method used. There's still a need for technical analysis, but the security lapse makes the task easier.

CODE-BREAKING TECHNOLOGY

Code-breaking doesn't usually take a climactic form. We don't see hours of frustrating work, with the crypto text suddenly giving up its secret at the end. More often, especially with complicated codes and ciphers, the work is slow and proceeds only by increments. Statistical analysis will reveal a pattern, but this will result in only a few elements of the message coming out. The technician must then poke and probe, trying various combinations, slowly teasing the message out letter by letter.

To break into an unknown message by cryptanalysis, it's necessary to find out how it was encrypted. The first step is to determine if the message is in code or cipher. This can be the most difficult part, because only the most simple-minded code-makers would produce an easily recognizable message. Let's look at a very simple message:

SDD NHGY FTG NKJKLHJ DRR

It's obvious that this is a substitution cipher. The different word lengths are the tip-off. On the other hand, if we see something like the following, we know that it's likely to be a transposition cipher:

$$
\begin{array}{cccccccc}
S & D & F & G & H & J & K & L \\
W & E & R & D & F & C & V & B \\
Y & U & H & J & J & K & N & M \\
L & K & J & H & G & F & F & D \\
I & U & Y & T & R & E & W & Q \\
\end{array}
$$

The block of letters is composed of five groups of eight letters each, and no code has eight-letter groups. There's simply no need.

Simple codes, if there's no attempt to disguise them, are in groups of five or six letters or numbers:

GHJKL RTYEW XCVBN GHJKL JHGFD FDSAW RFVGT YHNJU IKMJU IKUYH

There's no reason why the user of a transposition cipher can't break his message up into five-letter groups. A code-cracker can spend many frustrating hours trying to figure out the system without gaining an insight into the type used.

As we've seen, a cryptographer who wants to cause his rivals grief can superencipher his code groups.

The next step in technical code-cracking is to make a frequency count of the letters. We know that the most common letters in English are, in descending order of frequency:

ETAONRISH

The frequency count is, however, a statistical tool. What it means is that the longer the message, the better the odds of its frequency distribution being normal. Short messages can give trouble. Let's look at one which fits the rules:

COME HERE AT ONCE

This message has 4 "E"s, which is normal in the sense that "E" is the most common letter in English. Another short message might read:

DON'T COME NOW

In this one, there are three "O"s and only one "E." This throws off the usefulness of the frequency count.

For the best results, we need a fairly long message, or several in the same cipher. Assuming the language is English, we'll get something like this if it's a simple transposition cipher:

E -	618
T -	475
A -	400
O -	398
N -	352
R -	348
I -	320
S -	299
H -	248

This is a distribution frequency that follows the actual occurrence of these letters in English very closely. A safe move is now to try to dope out the pattern of transposition. This is often a lot of trial-and-error.

If it's a simple substitution cipher, we'll get a similar frequency distribution, but not for the same letters. Instead, it might look like this:

X -	618
G -	475
W -	400
L -	398
Y -	352
Z -	348
J -	320
K -	299
Q -	248

With such a distribution, a good starting point is to assume that "X" stands for "E," "G" stands for "T," etc.

There's another possibility. The cipher might be designed to suppress frequencies, as is the case with a polyalphabetical cipher. Then, the results might look like this:

X -	418
G -	460
W -	401
L -	375
Y -	365
Z -	368
J -	370
K -	399
Q -	348

This is a headache, because it suggests a polyalphabetic cipher. However, there is a way to crack this type of cipher. This is called the "Kasiski" method, named after a German officer who devised it in the middle of the Nineteenth Century. Let's look at a simple example:

Key: LOVELOVELOVELOVELOVELOVELOVELOVE
LOVELOVELOVELOVELOVELOVELOVE

Text: Thereisanotherproblemthatweshouldthinkaboutthistime-thatwehave

UGQMGFCAXZBWGWFMWNJ2YUNERRQLDZASIUNVXD VDWTBKDFCKCBQKDOBHGGVI

We see recurring patterns, such as "FC," "KD," and "UN." Working with these can give us the length of the key. The period, or separation, between the two instances of "FC" is 40. If we factor that, we get 5 and 8, and 4 and 10. The next one to analyze and factor is "UN." This gives us 12, which breaks down into 4 and 3. "KD" gives us 12 again, with the same factors. We find that "4" is the only factor common to all three, and therefore it's the most probable. It's not the only possibility, as the key word might have been one which has repetitions in it, such as "ONION." That would give some false leads to the length of the key word, but a little trial-and-error would reveal the true length.

Once we know the length of the key word, we know how many different ciphers are in the message, and we have to solve it remembering that only every fourth letter is in a particular substitution cipher. A practical point is that this cuts the sample size down to one-fourth, and this is why we need more text to construct an adequate frequency table. With a frequency table for each cipher, we can make some trial substitutions and start cracking the system.

UGQMGFCAXZBWGWFMWNJZYUNERRQLDZASIUNVXDVDWTBKDFCKCBQKDOBHGGVI
SDFGHJKLWERDFCVBYUHJJKNMCGYNJJWEEDCRFVYHJUJKUIKOLOLPLPTYHJNM
LKJHGFFDPOIJHGFBVXSREWREQRFDCWEDFVYFDZRTYJMUHGVCTYUJIUYTREWQ
QSXEDFVRFAZASZXEDEDRDFCRFEDUJKWSUJRDFCOLYHGFCPKJYIYGGOJFJFUF
YHJTFYHNTFDGBNVCXVBNMBVCXZVBDSGHJKREYUJKRFDYHEDIKEDIDJDUJIOW
WQQWESADFGSUJDSYHJFTYCBNSYHJSLWPISOKDOKDIUJSYHNESUJDILWSHUJS
EDGWFDJHJHVBTFDEFIJHUHGVYGEDIKJMWAIJMESGBNGFDYHKWYDHSJDGHDSH
ESYHIJRFDYHRFDSUHNGFDUHJNMHGFCOLGFPLYHGPLYGKKJSDBNMXHHGJHSSH
DJHEUEUYBCABKJHSDGAYUIBHJVCGARYUBVNMCBHJKHGSHIUGWSAPHJSTRGSS
WIGSPOUABNXZDFBKDWSAISFDJHKEWRYUFDKSGAHJDASSSDHJSDAFNBAHJSDH

One type of solution to the polyalphabetic cipher is called the "Kerckhoffs," after its inventor. The main value of the Kerckhoffs method is that it doesn't matter how long the key is. The technique is to stack several different messages enciphered with the same key. The result looks somewhat like the next example.

No matter what the key is, or how long it is, the first letter in each row has been enciphered with the same cipher alphabet. This simplifies the problem, because it means we can treat each column as a simple monoalphabetical substitution. As a practical matter, we can soon find several columns enciphered with the same alphabet, because few key words run over 12 letters.

There's another Kerckhoffs principle which can apply to alphabets derived with a keyword as a "primer." Let's look at an example of several such alphabets:

```
C O M P A N Y B D E F G H I J K L O Q R S T U V W X Z
O M P A N Y B D E F G H I J K L O Q R S T U V W X Z C
M P A N Y B D E F G H I J K L O Q R S T U V W X Z C O
P A N Y B D E F G H I J K L O Q R S T U V W X Z C O M
A N Y B D E F G H I J K L O Q R S T U V W X Z C O M P
```

We see that in each alphabet, each ciphertext letter is separated from the other by a spacing which does not change between different alphabets. For example, there are two letters between "A" and "B" in all of them. Likewise, we find three letters between "Q" and "U" in all of them. This provides a tremendous break for the cryptanalyst. When he starts working out a solution for one cipher, he's got a lead to the spacing on all of the others. This is what Kerckhoffs called "symmetry of position."[33] We can take warning from this in constructing our own ciphers. A randomly mixed alphabet, different for each cipher, will defeat the Kerckhoffs technique.

Yet another technique is laying out the message and writing the plain alphabets underneath it. This will bring out a message enciphered in a monoalphabetic or a polyalphabetic substitution, as long as it's enciphered in coherent alphabets.[34] Let's see how one message might come out.

RWNNMHXDLXVNJCXWLN

This is our ciphertext. We write it out and complete the alphabets below it:

```
R  W  N  N  M  H  X  D  L  X  V  N  J  C  X  W  L  N
S  X  O  O  N  I  Y  E  M  Y  W  O  K  D  Y  X  M  O
T  y  P  P  O  J  Z  F  N  Z  X  P  L  E  Z  Y  N  P
U  Z  Q  Q  P  K  A  G  O  A  Y  Q  M  F  A  Z  O  Q
V  A  R  R  Q  L  B  H  P  B  Z  R  N  G  B  A  P  R
W  B  S  S  R  M  C  I  Q  C  A  S  O  H  C  B  Q  S
X  C  T  T  S  N  D  J  R  D  B  T  P  I  D  C  R  T
Y  D  U  U  T  O  E  K  S  E  C  U  Q  J  E  D  S  U
Z  E  V  V  U  P  F  L  T  F  D  V  R  K  F  E  T  V
A  F  W  W  V  Q  G  M  U  G  E  W  S  L  G  F  U  W
B  G  X  X  W  R  H  N  V  H  F  X  T  M  H  G  V  X
C  H  Y  Y  X  S  I  O  W  I  G  Y  U  N  I  H  W  Y
D  I  Z  Z  Y  T  J  P  Y  J  H  Z  V  O  J  I  X  Z
E  J  A  A  Z  U  K  Q  X  K  I  A  W  P  K  J  Y  A
F  K  B  B  A  V  L  R  Z  L  J  B  X  Q  L  K  Z  B
G  L  C  C  B  W  M  S  A  M  K  C  Y  R  M  L  A  C
H  M  D  D  C  X  N  T  B  N  L  D  Z  S  N  M  B  D
I  N  E  E  D  Y  0  U  C  O  M  E  A  T  0  N  C  E
```

---

[33] *The Code-Breakers,* David Kahn, NY, MacMillan, 1967, p. 237.
[34] *Elementary Cryptanalysis,* Abraham Sinkov, Yale University, 1966, pp. 13-16.

87

- - - - - - - - - - - - - - - - - -

```
J O F F E Z P V D P N F B U P O D F
K P G G F A Q W E Q 0 G C V Q P E G
L Q H H G B R X F R p H D W R Q F H
M R I I H C S Y G S Q I E X S R G I
N S J J I D T Z H T R J F Y T S H J
O T K K J E U A I U S K G Z U T I K
P U L L K F V B J V T L H A V U J L
Q V M M L G W C K W U M I B W V K M
```

The message becomes very clear on one line. Note, however, that there are other words formed on various lines. We find "PULL" on the next to the bottom line, as we find "DIZZY" on the fifth line above the message and "OFF' on the line right below it. We know that the message is solved when we see coherent text all the way across, though. Single words don't count.

There are also other methods of analysis. At this point, let's introduce the paper slide, because we have to face the possibility that the cipher we're trying to break is a transposition cipher, and the slide is useful against either type. The slide means writing the unknown ciphertext onto strips of paper which we can place against each other in different positions. This is a trial-and-error method, but if we see a word emerge while we're sliding the paper strips, we know that we've got a break into a transposition cipher. We can also use the paper slide with the letters of the alphabet in order, to work the deciphering procedure outlined above.

THE KAPPA TEST

```
UGQMGFCAXZBWGWFMWNJZYUNERRQLDZASI UN.VXDVDWT'BKDFCKCBQKDOBHGGVI
SDFGHJKLWERDFCVBYUHJJKNMCGYNJJWEEDCRFVYHJUJKUIKOLOLPLPTYHJNM
LKJHGFFDPOIJHGFBVXSREWREQRFDCWEDFVYFDZRTYJMUHGVCTYUJIUYTREWQ
QSXEDFVRFAZASZXEDEDRDFCRFEDUJKWSUJRDFCOLYHGFCPKJYIYGGIJFJFUF
YHJTFYHNTFDGBNVCXVBNMBVCXZVBDSGHJKREYUJKRFDYHEDIKEDIDHDUJIOW
WQQWESADFGSUJDSYHJFTYCBNSYHJSLWPISOKDOKDIUJSYHNESUJDIKWSHUJS
```

| EDGWFDJHJHVBTFDEFIJHUHGVYGEDIKJWMAIJMESGBNGFDYHJWYDHSJDGHDSH |
| ESYHIJRFDYHRFDSUHNGFDUHJNMHGFCOLGFFLYHGPLYGKKJSDBNMXHHGJHSSH |
| DJHEUEUYBCABKJHSDGAYUIBHJVCGARYUBVNMCBHJKHGSHIUGWSAPHJSTRGSS |
| WIQSPOUABNXZDFBKDWSAISFDJHKEWRYUFDKSGAHJDASSSDHJSDAFNBAHJSDH |

FIGURE 12

The letters of an unknown encripted message are written onto long strips in order to use the Kappa Test to discover repeated characters.

This is strictly a statistical method, and its main use is to spot when a cipher alphabet repeats. This technique was devised by William Friedman, the American cryptanalyst who cracked the Japanese "PURPLE" cipher. Friedman realized that there are certain mathematical principles governing any effort at cryptanalysis. One of them is what he called the "Index of Coincidence." This means that the chances of getting pairs in chains of letters written randomly are .0385. To give a practical example, let's say that we have two lines of letters, one above the other, and that both are totally random. The chances of having two identical letters above each other are .0385.[35]

Now let's take the case of English text, in which letter frequency is not at random. In 1000 letters of English text, we'll find 130 "E"s and 80 "A"s, etc. The chances of finding identical letters with two superimposed texts is 0.0667. This means 6.67 for each I00 pairs of letters. This figure varies for each language, just as frequency count of letters does.

The practical value of the Kappa test is to discover the "period," or key length, of an unknown polyalphabetic cipher. It's helpful to write the letters of the unknown encryption out on strips, and to slide them over each other. This is simply a mechanical convenience to avoid having to write the text again for each trial.

---

[35] *The Code-Breakers*, pp. 376-384.

Let's take a couple of strips to see how the Kappa test works:

UGQMGFCAXWBWGWFMWNJZYUNERRQLDZASI UNVXDVDWT B KD F CKC BQKDOB IIGG VI
SDFGIIJKLWERDFCVBYUHJJKNMCGYNJJWEEDCRFVYHJUJKUIKOLOLPLPTYHJNM

We see that, out of 60 letter pairs, we have two cases of doubled letters, which works out to .033%. This fits the notion of simple coincidence. Now we take the two strips and slide the lower strip one space over:

UQMGFCAXWBWGWFMWNJ ZYUNERRQLDZ AS I UNVXDVDWTBKDFCKCBQKDOBHGGV I
SDFGHJKLWERDFCVBYUHJ "KNMCGYNJ JWEEDCRFVYHJUJKUIKOLOLPLPTYHJNM

We now find four pairs, or .066%. This suggests that the cipher alphabets are synchronized, and that we can proceed with multiple solutions by working down the columns of the ciphertext.

There's a catch. There always is. Much depends upon sample size. A short text is less likely to conform to the pattern than a longer one. Therefore, the figures you get when you try this may not be exactly right. In rare cases, you might obtain figures that show exactly the opposite. You have to work the odds, though, and go with the best chances, while remaining mentally prepared for the exceptional case.

There's yet another statistical test, known as the "phi," for finding whether a column in a stack is truly enciphered with the same alphabet. Let's say that we've got a stack fifty letters deep. We start by multiplying that number by the same number minus 1. This reads out to:

$$50 \times 49 = 2450$$

We take this and multiply it by our Kappa figure for polyalphabets, which is .0385, giving us 94.325. We then take the same figure and multiply it with our monoalphabetic Kappa, which is .0667, giving us 163.415. We then do a frequency count in the column or message. We take the total for each letter listed and multiply it by that number, minus 1. If we have 3 "A"s, for example, we don't square 3, we multiply it by 2, giving 6. We go through this for all of the letters listed. Let's say they are:

A	C	E	F	J	M	O	R	T	W	Z		
3	4	1	6	7	5	8	4	5	3	3	=	49
6+	12+	1+	30+	42+	20+	56+	12+	20+	6+	6	=	211

That's quite a bit over the 163.415 figure for a monoalphabetic cipher, which makes it almost a sure thing that this one is correctly stacked. Let's see how this procedure would shape up if there had not been as many high numbers in our count:

A	C	D	E	F	H	J	L	M	O	Q	R	S	T	V	W	X	Z		
3	2	1	3	3	2	3	3	2	3	4	3	3	1	3	3	3	4	=	50
6	2	O	6	6	2	6	6	2	6	1	6	6	0	6	6	1	1	=	10
+	+	+	+	+	+	+	+	+	+	2	+	+	+	+	+	2	2		2
										+						+	+		

102 is very close to our polyalphabetic figure, 94.325. If we get a result like this, we can safely assume that we don't have it stacked correctly, and we ought to try shifting one or more rows and do another test.

The chi test compares two messages, and can determine if they've been enciphered with the same key. You do this by counting the numbers of letters in each message, and multiplying them together. If you feel that the messages are monoalphabetic, you multiply the product by the monoalphabetic Kappa figure, which is .0667. This gives you the calculated chi for mono- alphabetic substitutions. You then multiply the same product by the lower figure, .0385, to give you a calculated chi for polyalphabetics.

The next step is to multiply the number of "A"s in one message by the number in the other. You do this for every letter, and add the results together. How do they compare with the two figures you've already worked out?

THE PLAYFAIR CIPHER: SPECIAL TECHNIQUES

As we saw from a previous chapter, the Playfair suppresses frequency count somewhat, and provides variable substitution according to each letter's neighbor in the pair. The Playfair is somewhat more tedious to dissect than a simple substitution, but it's vulnerable to analysis because it leaves its "fingerprint" on messages.

Several suggestive features help identify a Playfair. These aren't totally conclusive, but they point very strongly. One is that the frequency count is based on 25 letters, with usually the "I" or "J" missing. Another revealing feature is that a Kasiski superimposition shows only two alphabets in use. We also never find pairs consisting of doubled letters. Finally, the messages always have an even number of letters.

We have to change our thinking somewhat when working with a Playfair. We know that we're working with a two-letter "alphabet" of about 600 pairs. Likewise, the pattern of substitution is limited. In unraveling a Playfair, it's good to keep in mind that the system has certain weaknesses. A certain word has a 50-50 chance of having the same ciphertext, whatever its position in the message, whereas with a polyalphabetir substitution, it would be very rare that the same word would encipher exactly the same twice. This is one of the distinguishing characteristics that allow the code-breaker to tell that he's working with a Playfair. The only reason a certain word would generate a different ciphertext is that it might break into different pairs, according to its position in the message. For example, NEED could divide as "NE ED" or with the first and last letters as parts of other pairs: "-N EE D-." In any event, a word can encipher only two ways with a Playfair.

Another characteristic is that a pair substitution done on the diagonal will always be reciprocal. If "OG" stands for "TH," then "TH" also stands for "OG." Even a simple substitution cipher doesn't have this weakness. However, this doesn't work for letter pairs on the same line, vertical or horizontal.

Another characteristic is that, despite the theoretical possibility of over 600 pairs, each letter can have only those adjacent or diagonal as substitutes. Also important is that only letters in the same column or row as the high-frequency letters, ETAONRISH, will have high frequencies in the enciphered message.

LETTER PATTERNS

In English, as in any language, there are not only certain letters that occur more often than others, but certain combinations that predominate. For example, the combination "TH" occurs more often than any other. "HE" is the next most common, with "AN" and "IN" following. Likewise, three-letter combinations, or "trigraphs," also have their frequencies. "THE" is the most common, with "AND" and "THA" not far behind. There are also "contact frequencies," tables of probability of letters' being adjacent. For example, the letter "A" has "N" on its right side 21% of the time, and "H" on the left 14% of the time.[36]

The value of these contact tables comes after the initial break in the cipher. Statistical analysis can provide the locations of a few common letters, but the cryptanalyst must use common sense, intuition, and probability tables to dope out what letters precede or follow them. For example, the letter "E" may have emerged in this combination:

        Ciphertext: UGQMGFCAXWBWGWFMWN
        Cleartext: e e   e t   e

We know that this is our test message; "I need you. Come at once," but the code-breaker doesn't. He has a double E, and this is his first line of attack. There are only a few words using a double E, such as "MEET," "MEETING," and "NEED." The T also offers a clue, because the most likely letter on its left is "A," and the most likely letter to the right is "H." We know that "A" is correct, but the code-breaker will have to do it by trial and error. Cribbing from the message's context sometimes helps.

In the above ciphertext, words are not run together and chopped into groups of five. Let's see how much easier his task would be if the words were normally separated:

    Ciphertext: U GQMG FCA XWBW GW FMWN
    Cleartext: e e   e t   e

This is a good example of how even a simple message becomes very obscure when word length is eliminated. Word length and breaks are other aspects that the code-breaker has to reconstruct.

---

[36] *Cryptanalysis,* pp. 218-221. Also *Elementary Cryptanalysis,* pp. 175-179.

BREAKING TRANSPOSITION CIPHERS

Simple transpositions yield to trial and error. Paper slides often help provide a break into the pattern. The code-breaker has to consider every possibility, such as the letter order running up. down, diagonally, in a spiral, etc.

One technical aid is the paper slide. Writing the message vertically on strips of paper and pairing them in various orders gives test pairs. Checking these for likely digraphs helps find which columns belong next to each other.

With a transposition cipher, the code-breaker can gain a lot of help from cribs. Knowing the context of the message helps dope out some probable words. Anagramming locates the letters that make up probable words in the columns and rows of the ciphertext, and arranging the other letters to suit the pattern will bring out the rest of the message.

Having several messages enciphered with the same transposition cipher provides a tremendous advantage if there are repeated sequences between two or more messages. These can help force an entry into the cipher because they suggest that the same phrase or sentence is common to both messages. This characteristic cuts down the number of trial and error grids because it eliminates all in which the letters don't fit in the same relationship to each other.

Grills are somewhat harder to break, and the code-breaker depends a lot upon intuition, as in solving anagrams.

COMPUTERS FOR CRYPTANALYSIS

The first computers of the modern era were employed for cryptanalysis. During WWII, the British code-breaking establishment built several rudimentary computers to help them obtain the keys of the German "Enigma" cipher system. After the war, the British and American governments sponsored the development of new models of computers for code-breaking. Almost all of this is classified, and we don't know how many computers are at the National Security Agency.

THE NATIONAL SECURITY AGENCY

This super-secret agency has probably the world's best resources for code-cracking. It's generally known that the NSA has had computers for both code-making and code-breaking since its beginning in the late 1940s. If a cryptanalyst has a properly programmed "mainframe" computer, he can do at least the following tasks very quickly and easily:

Compile a list of the most common letters in a particular language and their frequency.

Compile similar lists for digraphs and trigraphs.

Compile a list of most commonly-used words in that language.

Compile similar lists for special traffic, such as a target country's military communications.

Analyze a message or group of messages for frequency count and other characteristics.

Run a phi and a chi on a message in every likely combination Run test decipherments at a speed far faster than any human operator.

Cross-match code groups against others, singly and in combination, to find matching clusters.

The exact capabilities of the computers at NSA and the uses they see are classified. However, knowing that modern "supercomputers" have phenomenal calculating speeds and memories, we can speculate. Supercomputers are already into their second generation at this writing, and a third will be along any day, with enhanced capabilities. The following tasks, if not quite possible with today's machines, soon will be:

Storing the texts, including page numbers, of every dictionary printed. This would allow running comparisons with intercepted code groups to determine if they correspond to coherent texts using these dictionaries.

Storing every message ever intercepted, and periodically making electronic comparisons to determine if they're in similar crypto-systems.

Making statistical comparisons of messages received in clear to determine if any correspond to encrypted texts in the computer's memory.

Another possibility is that a supercomputer can analyze ciphertext by running contact pairs, and make a start at restoring the plaintext, without a human operator's intervention. This is strictly a statistical method, and can be automated.

THE HOME COMPUTER

What about the code-breaker who has only a home computer? He can also do a few things, without fancy programming. to break codes and ciphers. One technique is to keyboard the batch of messages and stack them. Let's see what that can look like:

UGQMGFCAXZBWGWFMWNJZYUNERRQLDZASIUNVXDVDWTBKDFCKCBQKDOBHGGVI
SDFGHJKLWERDFCVBYUHJJKNMCGYNJJWEEDCRFVYHJUJKUIKOLOLPLPTYHJNM
LKJHGFFDPOIJHGFBVXSREWREQRFDCWEDFVYFDZRTYJMUHGVCTYUJIUYTREWQ
QSXEDFVRFAZASZXEDEDRDFCRFEDUJKWSUJRDFCOLYHGFCPKJYIYGGOJFJFUF
YHJTFYHNTFDGBNVCXVBNMBVCXZVBDSGHJKREYUJKRFDYHEDIKEDIDJDUJIOW
WQQWESADFGSUJDSYHJFTYCBNSYHJSLWPISOKDOKDIUJSYHNESUJDILWSHUJS
EDGWFDJHJHVBTFDEFIJHUHGVYGEDIKJMWAIJMESGBNGFDYHKWYDHSJDGHDSH
ESYHIJRFDYHRFDSUHNGFDUHJNMHGFCOLGFPLYHGPLYGKKJSDBNMXHHGJHSSH
DJHEUEUYBCABKJHSDGAYUIBHJVCGARYUBVNMCBHJKHGSHIUGWSAPHJSTRGSS
WIGSPOUABNXZDFBKDWSAISFDJHKEWRYUFDKSGAHJDASSSDHJSDAFNBAHJSDH

With a computer, it's possible to run through some manipulations that would take hours with pencil and paper. One example is sliding the message strips around in different orders to check for transpositions, as shown in Figure 13.

FIGURE 13

Using a computer, you can search for transpositions in a matter of seconds using only a few keystrokes. The highlighted trial shown above took only about 30 seconds.

Computer manipulation is also useful for stacking polyalphabetic ciphers to check for periodicity. A lot of this is trial and error, with a lot of time spent writing letters on paper. With a computer, it's only necessary to keyboard the texts once. Manipulation is then possible with only a few extra keystrokes.

There are cryptanalytical programs in BASIC for the home computer buff. These check a message for digraphs, trigraphs, index of coincidence, matching alphabets, and other characteristics. Although they're not a substitute for a gifted human cryptanalyst, these programs save many hours of donkey work.[37]

CONCLUSIONS

Code-breaking is both a science and an art. It depends upon both for cracking basic crypto-systems, but the code-breaker needs much more to crack high-security systems. Luck played a crucial part in many important cases. So did the availability of cipher machines on the open market, and the willingness to steal codes and ciphers when necessary. The amateur code- breaker's resources are limited, and a realistic appraisal suggests that he'll be better off finding his information by other means, if available.

---

[37] *Elementary Cryptanalysis*, pp. 193-222.

9

Quasi-Cryptosystems

There are several types of crypto-systems which aren't, strictly speaking, for secret transmission of information. Although not originally designed for coding, they offer some communication security as a by-product.

SQUIRT RADIO

"Squirt radio" sends a message at many times normal speed, sharply reducing transmission time and vulnerability to direction-finding. This technique originated with the German espionage services during WWII, and enabled their agents to send radio messages back to base with much reduced risk of being pin-pointed by triangulation.

Although the agent's messages were coded, squirt transmission wasn't to enhance message security. It helped protect the agent because radio-location techniques of the era required many minutes to carry out. When a direction-finding network detected an unknown or suspect transmission, it was necessary to alert at least two, preferably three, direction-finding stations to get a "fix" on it. For best results, these stations had to be many miles apart to give a good baseline for triangulation, and co- ordinating them required telephoning back and forth.[38]

---

[38] *Clandestine Operations,* Pierre Lorain, NY, MacMillan Publishing Company, 1983, pp. 28-42.

The old trick of transmitting on a frequency adjacent to an established transmitter no longer worked well because of the increased sophistication of detection devices. A central control station might have hundreds of cathode-ray tubes showing every transmitter in the spectrum, and any new ones would be immediately apparent, however close they were to the station supposedly shielding them.

The hardware for squirt transmission consists of a two-speed tape recorder and a radio transmitter. The operator turns his recorder on to slow speed, plugs it into his transmitter, and taps out his enciphered message, using his radio's morse key. He then rewinds his tape, turns the transmitter on, and raises home base. This takes only a few seconds if all goes well. He then runs the tape through at high speed. Depending on the length of the message, transmission takes only a few seconds, not enough for any "goniometric" receiver to get a fix on it. The operator al home base has a tape recorder set up to record the message al high speed. Playing it back at slow speed allows listening to the message.

The squirt transmitter isn't as effective today because of increasingly sophisticated and automated direction-finding equipment. Today's military have electronically interlocked direction-finding stations, where goniometric receivers scan the frequencies for unknown or suspect signals. When a receiver picks one up, it transmits a signal to the central computer, which commands other receivers at remote sites to search and record on that frequency. Direction-finding is almost instantaneous. Accuracy is enhanced because comparing azimuths is no longer the only way to locate the source of a signal. The computer compares relative signal strength from several receivers. Using an extremely precise clock, it can also compare the times the signal arrives at each receiver. Synthesizing the three techniques gives a very close approximation of the unknown transmitter's location, and much more quickly (only a couple of seconds) than was possible during WWII.

THE TRUNKING SYSTEM

Police agencies are getting squeezed in communication channels. Although the number and size of police agencies in this country is increasing, and so are the workloads, there is a finite number of radio channels available for police use. One way of handling the problem is "trunking" radio channels.

"Trunking" means that many channels are computer-squeezed onto a few radio frequencies. The central computer takes advantage of the "dead time" on each frequency. Normally, a frequency used for voice traffic doesn't have a voice on it every instant. There are periods of silence, but only a computer can monitor all of the available frequencies and pick up the dead time. When a police operator keys the microphone, the computer will scan all available frequencies, and when one is free, will transmit the conversation on it, switching it back and forth between frequencies as necessary, and inserting portions of other conversations when dead time develops on each channel.

An eavesdropper can listen in with a police monitor, a receiver tuned to the police frequencies, and hear a coherent conversation on any frequency. However, if more than one conversation begins, the computer will start shuffling them from frequency to frequency and the eavesdropper will have a hard time following a particular conversation. Although the trunking system is in no way a "scrambler," it serves the same purpose in frustrating the unsophisticated eavesdropper.

MULTIPLEXING

This commonly-used technique transmits several channels of communication on the same frequency. Multiplexing is an electronic mixing technique that sees commercial use in FM-stereo broadcasts, for example. Although multiplexing is only for squeezing more information into a limited band, it's more secure than ordinary FM because it requires a special receiver to listen in.

LIGHT PIPES

Photo-optic "light pipe" communication is practical, using glass-fiber optics and special amplifiers and receivers. This offers some security from eavesdroppers.

Electronic telephone communication travels along wires, which are easy to tap, or on microwave channels, also easy to intercept. It's not necessary to cut and splice a telephone wire to monitor the traffic. A magnetic induction coil will do the job without leaving a physical trace. Long-distance telephone communication using microwaves is not secure because a discreetly disguised antenna and receiver anywhere along the route will pick up the messages.

Light pipes are not total protection against eavesdropping, but they don't radiate energy that can be picked up with induction coils or antennas. A long-distance system using light pipes is somewhat more secure against interception.

AUTHENTICATION CODES

The only message an "authentication code" transmits is that the bearer or source is genuine. A bank official issuing a large-figure certificate of deposit will ask the client for his mother's

maiden name as an identifier. This is extra protection in case an
impostor tries to withdraw the funds.

Military units use authentication codes to verify that orders
are genuine. In certain critical installations, such as those
equipped with nuclear weapons, these codes are different every
day. The President of the United States has a 24-hour assign-
ment of warrant officers who carry the "football," a satchel
containing the authentication codes for nuclear attacks. These
"bagmen" travel with the President wherever he goes. At the
receiving end, officers in charge of launching nuclear weapons
carry cards with the authentication codes. Upon receipt of a
message, at least two officers must compare their codes and
agree that the message is genuine before they can act upon it.[39]

---

[39] *The Code-Breakers*, David Kahn, NY, MacMillan, 1967, p. 717.

10

Communication Security

When it becomes necessary to transmit secrets, it's vital not to compromise them by errors and carelessness. That's what this chapter's all about. It's as much a list of "do's" as it is a list of "don'ts." Communication security is extraordinarily difficult because it's not enough to be strong and prepared in a few ways. It's vital to be defensive at every point and in every direction.

One extraordinarily annoying fact about crypto-systems and their messages is that someone can steal them without leaving a trace, and without your becoming aware that they're no longer secure. This is because secrecy is intangible. Stealing a tangible object leaves its owner aware that it's gone, but tapping into a telephone line does not stop messages from getting through. Likewise, intercepting a radio transmission doesn't stop it or even alert the sender that someone else is listening.

At the outset, deciding on a security policy sets the stage for everything else. It's important to understand the nature of secrecy, and how telling more people a secret increases the risk of exposure. This means that any crypto-system should not be spread indiscriminately but only on a "need-to-know" basis. The same applies to physical assets, such as code and cipher books, pads, and papers.

SAFEGUARDING CRYPTO MATERIALS

Governments keep their cryptographic materials behind bars.

Code books and cipher machines are always in locked rooms, with only specially cleared persons allowed inside. In many cases, code rooms are electronically screened to prevent eaves-dropping. Current comes in through specially shielded cables, and transmissions are also specially protected. This is because, as we've seen, it's possible to obtain the key settings of cipher machines by tapping into telephone or electric power wires.

The more modest user of crypto materials, who doesn't have the resources of a government to back him, needs simpler methods. The basic technique for the small user is to keep a "low profile." While it would be ridiculous to deny that an embassy has crypto facilities, a typical home or office usually doesn't. The best policy is simply to keep it quiet.

If it's necessary to cross frontiers or otherwise run the risk of a search, any crypto material must appear totally unconnected with this purpose. Items such as one-time pads and secret inks aree poor choices because, if found, they're give-aways. A dictionary or other book used for coding is a good choice because it has an innocent purpose, and books of all sorts are very common.

If you're a businessman using cryptography, designate a special room or office for the task. Don't call it the "code room." Instead, call it the "special auditing office" or another un-interesting name. The room should be at the interior of the building, without windows or extra doors. Keep the door locked, and make one person responsible for the security of the room and materials it contains. There should always be a second layer of security, such as a locked desk or filing cabinet for storing both crypto material and messages.

Although it may seem convenient to have a copier inside the code room, don't. This makes it too easy to copy restricted material. While it's possible to place a lock on the machine, and have a rule that no copies are to be made without two employees present, this isn't easy to enforce. Yes, there are machines with counters, and there are ways of keeping logs of copies made and checking them against the machine's counter, but these systems aren't secure. They're too easy to bypass by falsification and only a massive audit would reveal the deception. The best, and simplest way is to keep all copiers outside the room. There, you can be sure that anything that goes on the copier will already have been paraphrased.

Another point is to dispose of carbon copies and worksheets securely. Much important information has come into the hands of unauthorized persons who poke through trash. A paper shred- der costs several hundred dollars. A cheaper way is to drop the paper into an incinerator or dispose of it in a fireplace, always stirring the ashes afterwards.

SECURITY OF PERSONNEL

If you're going to use secret communications, it's good policy to restrict knowledge to trustworthy people. The military arm their code clerks, but this isn't always practical or even necessary in civilian life. It's very unlikely that armed paratroopers will be dropping down onto your lawn to kidnap you or to steal your codes.

Although there's no danger of armed attack, carelessness, stupidity, and greed can cause as much damage. If you're running a business in which confidentiality is important, you need people who show loyalty, and who have the maturity to handle the responsibility. If you're in a highly competitive business, in which industrial espionage is common, don't rely on "employee screening" methods to weed out incompetent or dishonest applicants. Anyone whom you assign to operate crypto-systems should have a proven track record with your company. They should also have demonstrated good judgment and a sense of proportion. It won't do to bring friends in to see where they work, for example. They should also understand that talking too much about their jobs can compromise security.

COMPARTMENTALIZATION

The big risk in cryptography is that anyone who breaks your code or cipher may have access to all of your secrets. One way to avoid this is a system of strict compartmentalization. If you have several offices with which you must keep in touch, use a different crypto-system for each. This prevents anyone from unlocking the entire operation by cracking or purloining one code or cipher.

IMPORTANT DON'TS

We've seen how using a length of ciphertext allows the code-breaker to line up segments with paper strips or with a computer to make a mathematical analysis and pry open the system. It's evident that if the code-breaker has cleartext to go with the intercepted message, it will speed up his work and make it much easier. This is why these "don'ts" are so important:

Don't send a message in one code or cipher, then repeat it in clear. As we've seen, doing this provides a code-breaker a good crib to use against your crypto-system.

There's another important side to this type of security. Don't publish or release to a third party any material that's been transmitted to you in crypto without paraphrasing it. If you paraphrase it, you impede efforts at comparisons of texts, and avoid unwittingly giving away your crypto-system. If you're a businessman, you might establish a rule that anything leaving the code room must be paraphrased.

Don't transmit any text or documents given to you without paraphrasing them. Any such document could be a set-up, to enable a code-cracker to have the same text in clear and in your system for comparison. The exceptions are documents given you by trusted people in your organization.

Don't send part of a message in cipher and part in clear. This should be obvious, but many still do it. Sending a message such as "DFGH NHYU BFI DC TERRYVILLE." suggests to even a mediocre code-cracker that the message reads "WILL MEET YOU AT TERRYVILLE." Anyone with knowledge of your movements can confirm the meeting.

Don't send the same message in two different systems. This again allows comparisons which can unravel both systems. If you have to send the same message to parties using two different crypto-systems, paraphrase one message, or send it by courier.

Don't risk compromising your crypto-system for the sake of one message. If there's any problem with your crypto-system, correct it before transmitting any messages. Under no circumstances should you transmit in part crypto, part clear. It's better to sacrifice the secrecy of that message by transmitting only in clear, and safeguarding your crypto-system.

Don't use stereotyped expressions or boilerplate language. Using boilerplate results in sending the same message, or part of a message, to two different parties. We've already covered the disadvantage that brings.

Don't fail to change keys at proper intervals. What are proper intervals? There's no exact answer. If you have a large volume of traffic, you may wish to change keys each day. If volume is low, once a month should be enough. Much depends on the skill of any code-breakers you think you're facing, and how long it takes before the messages become obsolete. If the information you transmit loses value very rapidly, you may feel that no code-breaker can crack your system quickly enough for the information to be useful.

You're probably correct, but what about the next series of messages? Cryptanalysis brings many benefits down the road, and insights gained today will help break encrypted messages tomorrow.

Another point is to change at least the keys whenever a trusted employee with access to the crypto material or the messages leaves your employ. This is particularly true if the employee goes to work for the competition. You'll always have the nagging suspicion that confidential information was his ticket to the new job.

Don't fail to report the loss or compromise of a key, code, or cipher immediately, and to stop using that system.

Don't fail to keep at least one set of back-up keys, ciphers, or code on hand at all times, ready for use. The system in use may be compromised at any moment, and it's wise to have another ready to go.

TELEPHONE SECURITY

Security of telephone conversations, never good, has been declining during the past couple of decades. With many long-distance telephone conversations transmitted by microwave, they're accessible to anyone with the right equipment. Cellular phones are becoming popular, and these put even local calls on the air. So do portable phones available in electronic stores for under one hundred dollars. All of these are vulnerable to interception by our own and even foreign governments. Satellites

pick up conversations and relay them to their governments' elec-
ronic snooping offices on Earth. Computers scan the speech,
seeking certain key words which suggest that the conversations
may be worth the attention of a human operator.

Private snoopers, such as business rivals, have more modest
resources. They're limited to tapping a line, and one fairly good
way of foiling this is to use a public phone for each end of the
conversation. Each party keeps a list of numbers of public
telephones that are conveniently near. Each one is numbered. To
avoid disclosing that a private conversation's about to take place,
there should be no mention of using a public phone. Instead one
party telephones the other and says something like: "How about
meeting me for a drink at five?" or, "I can't make our meeting
because I have to pick up my car at five." or, "We'll be able to
meet because I'm going to make sure to leave the office right at
five."

"Five" is the critical word. This signifies the number of the
telephone which the calling party will dial at a pre-arranged interval after he hangs up. If this is unsatisfactory, the other person
replies with another number, again working it into a sentence to
make it appear to be an innocuous conversation: "I can't make it
then. How about six?" or, "I thought you said your car wouldn't
be ready till six." or, "That's good. I usually leave around six, but
I'll cut it short tonight."

This tells the caller to dial listing number 6 at the proper time,
instead of phone number 5.

SCRAMBLERS

We've already covered these in a previous chapter, but here
we have to consider the practical aspects. First, scramblers are
expensive. You can expect to pay several hundred dollars for the

cheapest set. A scrambler is useless unless the other party has one, too. This means that their usefulness is very limited, as you can't just dial anyone you know and have your conversation scrambled.

Scramblers also vary in reliability. Keep in mind that both the transmitting scrambler and the receiver have to be synchronized to pass speech properly, and that often the synchronization slips. This is a surprisingly persistent problem, especially with the cheaper sets.

DISCRETION

The simplest defense against electronic snooping is discretion. Don't say anything on the phone that you don't want splashed over the front page of your local newspaper the next day. This is an overly dramatic way of phrasing it, but it stresses the importance of avoiding discussion of sensitive information.

POCKET CODES

A "pocket code" is a short list of code words or a cipher grid that will fit into a wallet. Ideally, it shouldn't be bigger than a 3" x 5" card, which can fold over once for compact carrying. However, a standard sheet of paper will also do if there are many code phrases to communicate, but it will be slightly more awkward.

In constructing a pocket code, there must be the same close attention to good practice as when compiling a major code or cipher. It's a serious mistake to use only fragments of code inserted into sentences. For example, the sentence "I'm going to meet Challenger at Grand Central Station at five o'clock" tells the listener that a meeting is about to take place, where it will be, and at what time. The only question is "Challenger's" identity.

It's far better to have entire sentences or meanings together:

ABLE	I am going to meet
ACTION	I need to meet
ADMIRE	We must go to
BAKER	John Smith
BASKET	Robert Smith
BISHOP	John Jones
CAT	At home
COW	At the airport
CROW	At the office
DOG	This is urgent
FERRET	This is not urgent
GOOSE	Come here at once
GRAVEL	Noon
HAPPY	One o'clock
HUT	Two o'clock
JOKE	Three o'clock
LEATHER	Four o'clock
LEAP	Five o'clock
LOVE	Six o'clock
MAN	Seven o'clock
MOP	Eight o'clock
NICE	Nine o'clock
OPERA	Ten o'clock
ORPHAN	Eleven o'clock
PANTS	Twelve o'clock
PRETTY	A.M.
PUTTY	P.M.
QUEER	As soon as possible

| QUIET | Will wait for reply |
| QUICK | Have... contact me |

The list covers enough possibilities to show how a pocket code can work to hide the meaning from an eaves- dropper. A longer code can cover more ground but will be harder to use quickly.

The pocket code requires the same sort of security that applies to other codes. It belongs in the wallet and on the person at all times. Leaving it in a desk, glove compartment, or hotel room provides opportunities for its loss or compromise.

RADIO

It's occasionally necessary to use some form of two-way radio in business and in our personal affairs. While it's unlikely that someone we want to avoid will be listening at exactly the moment we transmit, we should still observe discretion. Using a Citizens' Band channel or the Commercial Band doesn't make much difference regarding security. The only difference is that there's much less chance of interference from private citizens "talking trash" on the Commercial Band.

Using guarded speech and perhaps a pocket code will enhance security on the air, but it's important to avoid transmitting any information that doesn't absolutely have to go at that moment. If it can wait for a face-to-face meeting, it's better to avoid saying it.

If the matter's very urgent, it may be possible to use a landline, or public telephone. Granted, these aren't very secure, but using a phone for a brief message is usually better than putting sensitive information on the air. Using pre-arranged public phones offers the best hope. An office or home telephone might be tapped.